THE ATLANTIC CRITICAL STUDIES

ANITA DESAI'S

Fire on the Mountain

RAMA KUNDU

ATLANTIC

PUBLISHERS & DISTRIBUTORS (P) LTD

Published by
ATLANTIC
PUBLISHERS & DISTRIBUTORS (P) LTD
7/22, Ansari Road, Darya Ganj, New Delhi-110002
Phones : +91-11-40775252, 40775214, 23273880, 23275880
Fax: +91-11-23285873
Web: www.atlanticbooks.com
E-mail: orders@atlanticbooks.com

Printed & bound in India by Atlantic Print Services

General Preface

The Atlantic Critical Studies, modelled on the study-aids available in England and America, among other places, are primarily meant for the students of English literature of Indian universities.

However, in consideration of the local conditions and the various constraints under which our students have to study—non-availability of relevant critical books, dearth of foreign and Indian journals, inaccessibility to good, well-equipped libraries, just to mention a few of them—the models have been considerably improved upon, both qualitatively and quantitatively.

Thus, while these Studies are meant to be compressive and self-sufficient, the distinguished scholars who have prepared these study materials, have taken special care to combine lucidity and profundity in their treatment of the texts.

The Select Bibliography at the end is meant not only to acknowledge the sources used but also to help a student in the pursuit of further studies if s/he wants to.

Atlantic Publishers & Distributors believe in quality and excellence. These studies will only reconfirm it.

MOHIT K. RAY
Chief Editor [English Literature]
Atlantic Publishers & Distributors
New Delhi

Contents

1

Introduction

In an interview of 2001 Anita Desai had been asked by Magda Costa to comment on the contemporary literary scenario of India, *vis-à-vis* the comparative position of literatures written in the vernacular and in English respectively. The question was, "What do you think is the future of literature in Indian languages, now that Indian literature in English has become so strong?" Desai replied:

> It's become strong in the last ten or twenty years. When I started to write it certainly wasn't. There was just a few of us who were writing in English; we had a lot of problems in finding publishers, there were very few readers, and no one seemed very interested at all in our work. I think things changed very dramatically—and I can put a date to it: it was 1980—when Salman Rushdie published *Midnight's Children*, and it had such a huge success in the West. I think in India also. Readers and publishers took notice of it. After that there was a whole new wave of new writers. I think it was the success of his book that gave them such confidence, encouraged them to write. I think we all need models, and he was a model for that whole generation in the 80s. Also it is a growing confidence in the English language. When I started to write there was a lot of questioning: can you really express the Indian experience, and Indian ways of thinking and speaking in the English language—a foreign language? But I think by the 80s everyone accepted the fact that English had become an Indian language, it was not going to disappear, it had taken roots and had started growing not in any artificial manner but in a very natural manner. Indians have taken it to our world and turned it into an Indian language. So now they are writing with a kind of confidence. I think

> it is not questioned any more. I was always questioned about using English and I no longer am. I don't think my daughter has ever been questioned about it. There was a certain amount of resentment by writers in the Indian languages, because of all the attention it has received in the West [...].

Postcolonial Writing and Women

Postcolonialism, especially at its initial phase, is an assertion of cultural nationalism. This involves foregrounding indigenous views, tradition, and culture. Again, postcolonialism, particularly its early waves, involved the assertion of a voice which had remained unheard so long, the voice of people who were underdogs till the other day. Thus, it is a literature of the woman, of the black, of the various other formerly colonized ethnic segments of a people. This has often led to a paradoxical phenomenon in the case of emergent women writers in the ex-colonies. Excepting the case of settler colonies like those of Canada, Australia, or partly South Africa, the hold of tradition had been, and still is, strong in the frontiers of the former. Empire. This had of course positive sides; nevertheless, these traditions, deeply embedded as these were in age-old patriarchal mores and ideology, were found constricting by the emerging women writers of the postcolonial era.

Indian Women Novelists since the '50s

The post-fifties India witnessed the emergence of a number of major women writers in English. Kamala Markandya made her mark with *Nectar in a Sieve* in 1954. Ruth Jhabvala's *To Whom She Will* came out in 1955. Nayantara Sahgal's *A Time to be Happy* appeared in 1958. Among other women novelists who came in the wake and made their mark in recent years you can mention Bharati Mukherjee, Shashi Deshpande, Shobha De, Kamala Das, Namita Gokhale, Rama Mehta, Gita Mehta, Githa Hariharan, Bapsi Sidhwa, Manju Kapur, Arundhati Roy, *et al.*

The novels of Anita Desai can be studied against the above background. Among this galaxy of writers Anita Desai has proved herself to be a significant and prolific novelist who has curved out a special niche for herself. Anita Desai's novels epitomize the emerging women's search for self-hood in the Indian context.

She illustrates the Indian women writers' attempt, especially since the historical turn of our country by the mid-twentieth century, to give articulation to the women's own unique feelings and quests, aspirations and agonies,— an act which necessarily means challenging some basic tenets of their culture and tradition.

Anita Desai belongs to the generation of novelists on the Indian English scene who rose to prominence since the seventies, the previous three decades having been dominated by the 'Big Three' among others.

Anita Desai

Anita Desai was born in 1937, in Missouri, a hill station of India, of a Bengali father and a German mother. Her father was D.N. Mazumdar, a Bengali businessman, and mother was Toni Nime, a lady of German origin. Anita started writing in English quite early, at the age of seven, and published her first story at the age of nine. The girl was educated in Delhi at Queen Mary's Higher Secondary School and Miranda House, and received her graduation in 1957. In the following year she married Ashvin Desai, a businessman; they had four children.

Since the 1950s Anita Desai has lived in various cities of India, including New Delhi, Calcutta, Bombay, among others. She has received such recognition as membership of the Advisory Board for English of the National Academy of Letters in Delhi and a membership of the American Academy of Arts and Letters. She has also been abroad on teaching assignments at Girton College and Smith College in England, and at Mount Holyoke College in the United States. 1993, however, came as a turning point in Anita Desai's life when she got the job of a creative writing teacher at Massachusetts Institute of Technology. Since then she has been staying there for one semester each year while spending the rest of the year in India. Desai has also been felicitated as a Fellow of the Royal Society of Literature in London, in addition to receiving the Guardian Award for Children's Fiction for the novel *The Village by the Sea* (1982), and the 1978 National Academy of Letters Award for *Fire on the Mountain*. She has also been awarded the Literary Lion Award in 1993, and been nominated Helen Cam Visiting Fellow, Ashby fellow, and Honorary fellow of the University of Cambridge.

Apart from her eleven novels, Anita Desai has also written a number of short stories, stories for children, and articles. Some of her major titles are:

- *Cry, the Peacock,* 1963
- *Voices in the City,* 1965
- *Bye-Bye, Blackbird,* 1971
- *The Peacock Garden,* 1974
- *Where Shall We Go This Summer?,* 1975
- *Cat on a Houseboat,* 1976
- *Fire on the Mountain,* 1977
- *Games at Twilight and Other Stories,* 1978
- *Clear Light of Day,* 1980
- *Village by the Sea,* 1982
- *In Custody, 1984* [film 1993, dir. by Ismail Merchant, starring Shashi Kapoor, Shabana Azmi, Om Puri, screenplay by Anita Desai]
- *Baumgartner's Bombay,* 1988
- *Journey to Ithaca,* 1996
- *Fasting Feasting* 1999
- *Diamond Dust,* 2000 is her collection of stories.

Anita Desai started her writing career with short stories. The stories highlight some of the themes which go on recurring in her novels: the problem of women and children, of human relationships, of the oppression of the innocent and suffering of the fine under insensitive and brutal people and forces.

Anita Desai's debut novel *Cry, the Peacock* (1963) was published in Britain by Peter Owen, who is known for the titles he has published in literature of the British Commonwealth and continental Europe. *Cry, the Peacock* is a tragedy of mismatch, and consequent marital discord and psychological dislocation. Maya, an excitable girl with innate longing for joy and love, is married to the pragmatic, cold Gautam. She becomes increasingly alienated and disoriented until a time comes when she, under a frantic obsession with the peacock's cry, gives a fatal push to Gautam which kills him.

Cry, the Peacock was followed by *Voices in the City* (1965), which is located in the city of Calcutta. It is a story about three siblings—who had spent their childhood in a hill station on the

Himalayas, and came to Calcutta later on. Calcutta affects their lives in intricate ways, and one of them, Monisha, is destroyed by her stifling claustrophobic life in the household of a wealthy, old, and gross Calcutta family.

In *Where Shall We Go This Summer?* (1975) Sita, a mother pregnant with her fifth child, seeks to escape from a reality she finds too much to bear with. She takes refuge from the city and from her family and friends and husband in the island of her childhood in the abandoned homestead of her deceased father.

Fire on the Mountain (1977) is a beautiful novel, occasionally reaching lyrical heights; it is set in Kasauli, a hill station, and is focused on two elderly ladies and one small girl. Nanda Kaul in *Fire on the Mountain* retires to a hill station house in her old age, and leads an isolated life there, when her great-granddaughter arrives and comes to stay. With the arrival of Raka the story takes a new turn, gathers a momentum, and unfurls quickly to a symbolic end when the mountain has been set on fire.

Clear Light of Day (1980) is woven round the story of a middle-class Hindu family, set against the historical backdrop of Delhi. Bim or Bimla Das is a professor of history and an independent woman. But Bim is haunted by memories of the past as she goes about her daily life in the decaying family mansion in Old Delhi. Bim has a sister Tara, who does not understand Bim's resistance to change. The traumatic memory of partition—in the national history and the family history— continues to dominate the consciousness of the characters.

In *In Custody* (1984) Desai looks at literary traditions and academic illusions with a mild touch of irony. The story evolves around Nur, an once prosperous Urdu poet, who is now nearly pauperised, and Deven, the Hindi teacher in a backwater college, who is made to encounter the shocking disparity between his illusions about a beloved poet and the not-so-pleasant reality about the supposedly 'magical genius' of his imagination.

Critics have tried to read autobiographical meanings into *Baumgartner's Bombay* (1988), since the author's own parent was of German origin and her first language was German. It is the story of a Jewish businessman who had come to India in his youth in order to escape the Nazis, but continued to live here in poverty and isolation. The stray cats seem to be his sole companions. "His eyes were short-sighted and blinked half-shut against the glare that thrust itself in at the door and so he did not notice that watchman's expression as he passed him on his perch under the wooden board that bore the tenants' names—Hiramani, Taraporevala, Barodekar, Coelho, da Silva, Patel—mumbled 'Good morning, *salaam'*, and went down the steps into the street with his bag, uncertain as ever of which language to employ. After fifty years, still uncertain, Baumgartner, *du Dummkopf."* The monotonous peace of Baumgartner's life is shattered with the arrival of a German hippie.

Journey to Ithaca (1995) is a case apart in the Desai canon. It is, in a sense, a story of pilgrimage, reifying once again the once popular European paradigm of 'Journey to the East.' Three characters—Matteo and Sophie, the young Italian couple, and 'Mother,' a mysterious woman from across the seas in search of a 'guru'—make this pilgrimage. Ithaca here serves as a metaphor for India, or the destination for the spiritual seeker.

Fasting, Feasting (1999) highlights American and Indian cultures, as well as male and female roles as thematic counterpoints. It is the story of Uma and Arun, the sister and the brother from a middleclass Indian family in a small provincial city. Whereas Uma is denied any chance to be and become, Arun gets the chance to study in Massachusetts. Uma stays back in India with her parents whom she calls 'MamaPapa.' "It was hard to believe they had ever had separate existence, that they had been separate entities and not MamaPapa in one breath [...]. MamaPapa themselves rarely spoke of a time when they were not one. The few anecdotes they related separately acquired great significance because of their rarity, their singularity." Ironically, neither of the siblings finds happiness or fulfilment in their respective life-pattern.

India on the Writer's Agenda

While talking on the portrayal of the American way of life in *Fasting, Feasting* Anita Desai claimed and insisted:

> It was partly a response to all the literature that has been written by British authors about India. I felt it's about time that Indians, who now live in large numbers in the Western world, start writing about them too. It was about a foreigner's experience, not really an emigrant's experience like Bharati Mukherjee's characters. It was more about the fact that, no matter where you travel,

> you come across the same emotional hungers and needs. What is different is our ways of satisfying them. If you have nothing else in the world at least you have religion. In America people might think that a trip to the shopping mall is best.

At the same time on the other hand, the author believes that India offers a kind of inclusivity. In the interview with Magda Costa Desai spoke of her mother:

> [...] my mother adapted so completely to the Indian way of life that nobody thought of her as a foreigner anymore.

Perhaps this childhood memory worked behind her notion of Indian inclusivity. During the same interview she said:

> Indians manage to slip back and forth between the modern world, with a great ease, without feeling any strain. If there's one characteristic of India it is that it's very inclusive; it's not exclusive.

However, writing on India is not her agenda. On being asked by her interviewer, "What are your aims as a writer?" Desai said:

> I don't have an agenda as a writer. People think that because I write about India I must be trying to portray India in a way. But, really, when you write you don't think about your readers at all; you don't imagine what your readers will look for or what they expect from a book.

Here she comes to something fundamental about the act of writing itself. What she says brings to our mind the postmodern metafictional concept of the writer being a player, and the act of writing being the play.

> [...] [when you write] you are alone with that page and with your pen. You are really only playing a game by yourself: of imagining thoughts and images with the best words suitable. It's an exploration of language: how much can language do, or how far can it pretend human experience and feelings.

According to the commonly held critical opinion Anita Desai's novels show a tragic view of people. In this connection Desai tells Magda Costa:

> A lot of people tell me my books are extremely pessimistic, and extremely dark, but I would prefer to think of them as facing the truth, not having illusions.

Critical Response

N.R. Gopal, in his book on Anita Desai places the author in the tradition of Indian English writing and especially among the women writers at work, and thus helps us to see Anita Desai in perspective; Gopal writes:

> In order to place Anita Desai in proper perspective it is necessary to see her along with the other women novelists who have more or less the same thematic concern and who in their own way deal with the commonly shared theme of human relationship. All of them are chroniclers of the tension in the wake of India's emergence as a developing nation. For a better and easier understanding of this aspect of modern Indian women fiction writers in English we may look for general tendencies which unmistakably point towards certain commonly shared themes in their fiction.
>
> One of the themes recurring in the novels written during the post-Independence decades is the individual's nostalgia in treating the joint family. Often the central figures in the novels, in order to seek their own identities consciously, try to break away from the kind of life they are nostalgic for. The institution of the joint-family gives opportunity for group human behaviour, it symbolises an expansive pre-industrial way of life; and it represents a deeply entrenched form of orthodoxy against which the individual may find himself helpless. It gives way to presenting the conflict between two sets of values—one standing for the supremacy of social hierarchy and the other for that of the individual.
>
> The treatment of the theme by women novelists is a three-faceted affair. A personal story slowly develops into a wider conflict in which are involved the individual's identity for supremacy and the social demands. The personal story thus is used as a springboard to explore social change in India in all its complex manifestations. They seem to examine the transition from a traditional society to an urban industrial metropolitan society in its comprehensiveness.
>
> The comparative achievement of Anita Desai becomes clear when we notice that her fellow women writers like

Kamala Markandeya. Ruth Jhabvala, Nayantara Sehgal, Shanta Ramarao and Atiya Hussain seldom try to portray the psychic elements involved in these themes in their fullness. The tensions and anxieties of being modern in a traditional society have been overlooked by most of these writers who have mainly devoted their attention to broad social features that emerge in the course of gradual metamorphosis of the old order. So intense is their devotion to the physical aspects of this change that they fail to take note of and project the psychological reality which must, of necessity, be allowed an upper hand in the face of the world undergoing a rapid change with the advancement of scientific and technological knowledge and rapid progress of communication and industrialisation.

Anita Desai adds a new dimension to English fiction by concentrating on the exploration of this troubled sensibility a typical modern Indian phenomenon. In contrast to her in Jhabwala's work the social background is rather more important than the characters, in Kamala Markandeya's works the emphasis is as much on the principal characters as on matters—economic, political, social and cultural. Nayantara Sehgal while dealing with social problems, confines herself to a particular social class, namely the upper class and the aristocracy Anita Desai thus clearly stands ahead the group in as much as she introduces a shift of ideational focus from the outer to the inner part of human existence. Her novels focus on the inner climate, the climate of sensibility. Her main concern is to depict the psychic states of her protagonists at some crucial juncture of their lives. To sustain her effort she has forged a style supple and suggestive enough, to convey the fever and fretfulness, to record the eddies and currents in the stream of consciousness of her characters. The interplay of thought feelings and emotions is reflected in language, syntax and imagery [...]. (Gopal 4-5)

2

Fire on the Mountain: The Text

Story-Outline

Nanda Kaul, the elegant widow of the Vice-Chancellor, retires in her old age to the hill station resort of Kasauli mountain, in an old house once built and dwelt in by British expatriates, and left behind after 1947. Arrived here at last, she seems to have found a place of her own for which she had craved all her life. She lives here all by herself, and maintains a stoic posture of proud indifference to the rest of the world. She does not want to have any connection with the plains below where she had lived in the past, and where her friends and relatives continue to live. She does not want to remember the past. She does not even want any letter or message from this world. Still a message comes. It is a letter from her daughter Asha, who just thrusts her granddaughter upon the old lady without even seeking her consent. Nanda Kaul feels deeply annoyed that she should be thus called to take responsibility once again. There was a time when she had done everything for everybody in the large family. But now she wants her own peace.

Anyway, by the time she receives the letter it is already too late. Raka, Nanda Kaul's great-grandchild, and the child of a broken home, is already on the way. Raka's mother Tara, who happens to be the daughter of Asha, and granddaughter of Nanda Kaul, had repeatedly come to the point of breakdown under the pressure of an unbearable conjugal life. But Asha, as in earlier times, persuades Tara once again to have a try to make it up with her husband. This time they have got a chance of going abroad together. Since Raka has just recovered from serious illness, and more importantly, is supposed to be redundant on this make-up trip of her parents, she is packed up and sent to Carignano by her own grandmother to the grandmother's mother.

With Raka's arrival at Carignano things begin to change for Nanda Kaul. Raka, who is remarkably withdrawn and self-dependent for her age, loves the place at first sight. She moves about freely and alone on the mountain. Though initially Nanda Kaul was annoyed at the thought of fresh responsibilities and loss of privacy, now she increasingly realises day-by-day her own affinity with the child. As result involvement begins once again.

In order to amuse the child and keep her withindoors during a spell of bad weather Nanda Kaul starts spinning stories about her own past. This past includes her childhood in her father's house, and her married life in her husband's house. She fantasises the past in order to make it interesting to the child. But the child is uneasy and uncomfortable. She senses something wrong.

In the meantime Nanda Kaul is visited one afternoon by Ila Das. Ila Das and Nanda Kaul have been friends since their girlhood. Ila Das's father had spent all his savings and more for his sons' education abroad, and it was all lost upon them. But as result, Ila, her sister and her mother were left destitute. Ila Das has no one to fend for her; she is old, weak, suffering from extreme penury. Ila Das's suffering is, furthermore, accentuated by her upbringing as a lady. For a time in the past she had got some temporary job through the good offices of Nanda's husband. That period is treasured in Ila Das's memory as one of the happiest of her life. Now, in her old age Ila Das has no respite or retirement. Just for survival she has to continue in the ill-paid and hazardous job of a professional social worker. The very nature of her profession brings Ila Das into contact with the local society, along with its many events of child marriage. Ila Das feels disturbed by this practice of giving small girls in marriage to quite elderly men. She tries in vain to persuade the parents of the helpless victims, and does not know that in course of this work she has invited the wrath of one Preet Singh, a notorious man of the locality, who had struck a deal with an old man. Preet Singh had arranged the marriage of his seven years old daughter to a senile groom in exchange of a piece of land. Ila Das tries to persuade Preet Singh against the marriage.

It is around this time that Ila Das pays her visit to Nanda Kaul one afternoon, since her present posting happens to be within the same zone, in the village down the hills. After having tea with her friend Ila Das trudges back when it is already dark in the valley.

As she reaches the last rock on her road, a black shape detaches itself from the jagged pile of stones, and springs on her. Ila Das is raped and strangled by Preet Singh on her lonely way back home from Carignano at the day's end.

The news comes to Nanda Kaul as a rude shock and she is jolted into the self-perception that all the glittering stories she had yarned all these days were false, and that her true identity lay with Ila Das, the humiliated and mutilated woman.

The shock of the perception kills her. She dies while holding the telephone receiver.

In the meantime Raka has come back from her evening escapade into the mountains with the news that she has set the mountain on fire. But her *Nani* cannot answer her call. The novel ends with the fire raging through the woods and ravines, crackled around the dry wood and through the dry grass, and black smoke spiralling up over the mountain.

The title of the novel alludes to this closing event.

The Title

The title of the novel calls back to the title of the second chapter of William Golding's celebrated novel *Lord of the Flies* (1954).

In Golding's novel too the fire on the mountain, lit by children, has been used with rich ironic and symbolic suggestions. Some English children who got accidentally landed in a remote coral island on the Pacific decided to keep a small fire burning on the hill top so that the emanating smoke could attract some passing ship in the far sea, and thus they would be rescued. But in their over-enthusiasm the children lit up too huge a fire, which destroyed a portion of the flora and fauna of the island. Furthermore, it was also suspected that some of the smaller children might have been killed by the fire.

Anyway, at the initial stage the devastation was accidental. But at the end again we find there is a huge fire spreading through the entire island, and this time it has been intentionally lighted by some of the boys in order to capture and kill one of their fellows.

Anita Desai, however, seems to have used the phrase here—though it is a phrase resonant with associations of Golding's novel—with altogether different and ambiguous suggestions. Initially, mountain-fires of the past are hinted at; fires which had broken out on the mountains in the past years, recent or remote, and have left their mark on the charred pine tree trunks, or on the ruins of the burnt house on the hill. Such fires are common during summer, and are easily spread by a strong wind, as Ram Lal tells Raka. There is no choice for the people but to let it burn itself out since there is no adequate water on the hills to quench such fires. Eventually, Raka has the experience of seeing one real fire on the mountain, though from a distance of miles. Finally, at the end, the child herself sets the mountain on fire. Thus the novel also marks a process by which the fire comes closer by degrees across miles and years until it leaps into visible and audible proximity at the end. As the book closes, one can as it were see, hear, and even feel the heat of the very real fire, Raka's fire on the mountain.

> Down in the ravine, the flames spat and crackled around the dry wood and through the dry grass, and black smoke spiraled up over the mountain.

3

A Critical Summary of the Text

The Three Parts

Fire on the Mountain has been planned in a clear pattern of three parts. Each of these three parts is concerned with one of the three women characters in the novel, as is indicated by the three subtitles: 'Nanda Kaul at Carignano,' 'Raka Comes to Carignano,' 'Ila Das leaves Carignano.' The subtitles, simple as they are, unambiguously highlight the respective foci.

The first part shows Nanda Kaul at Carignano. In the following sections Raka and Ila Das increasingly inch forward to the front stage. The novel unfolds slowly through a crisscrossing between the present and the past, the uneventful mundane present and a supposedly glamorous past, between reality and reminiscence. It is only at the end, in the last but one page that the narrative takes a sharp turn, and leads to a vital disclosure about the past. This helps us to perceive and understand Nanda Kaul in a new light. Several hours after Ila's departure from Carignano there is a telephone call for Nanda Kaul. She is told over phone about the rape and murder of Ila Das, and is requested to "come to the police station at the earliest and identify [...]."

> But Nanda Kaul had ceased to listen. She had dropped the telephone. With her head still thrown back, far back, she gasped. No, no, it is a lie! No, it cannot be. It was a lie—Ila was not raped, not dead. It was all a lie, all. She had lied to Raka, lied about everything. Her father had never been to Tibet—he had bought the little Buddha from a traveling pedlar. They had not had bears and leopards in their home, nothing but overfed dogs and bad-tempered parrots. Nor had her husband loved and cherished her and kept her like a queen—he had only done enough to

> keep her quiet while he carried on a lifelong affair with Miss David, the mathematics mistress, whom he had not married because she was a Christian but whom he had loved, all his life loved. And her children—the children were all alien to her nature. She neither understood nor loved them. She did not live here by choice—she lived here alone because that was what he was forced to do, reduced to doing. All those graces and glories with which she had tried to captivate Raka were only a fabrication: they helped her to sleep at night, they were tranquillizers, pills. She had lied to Raka. And Ila had lied too. Ila, too, had lied, had tried. No, she wanted to tell the man on the phone. No, she wanted to cry, but could not make a sound. Instead, it choked and swelled inside her throat. She twisted her head, then hung it down, down, let it hang. (145)

PART I

Chapter 1

As the novel opens we see Nanda Kaul, as an aged woman standing under the pine trees at Carignano, 'her home on the ridge,' her hill-top house on Kasauli. She is aged but still very beautiful, self-consciously graceful and straight in her bearing. While pausing under the trees she is enfolded by the scented sibilance of the pine trees, and the invisible music of cicadas. But then her peace is ruffled as she spots the postman slowly winding up along the Mall route to the house. She is annoyed at the prospect of receiving letters; she is even irritated and wishes he did not stop.

The postman, with his fat bag of letters, messages and queries seems to be a harbinger of requests and demands from the plains, and Nanda Kaul does not want to have anything from the plains. She wants to be left alone. Anything or anybody coming up from the plains or the past to disturb her peace here is unwelcome.

Since she cannot stop the postman she tries, pathetically for a moment, to hide herself behind the pine branches. Tall and thin, in her grey sari, Nanda Kaul fancies as if she had merged into the tree. 'To be a tree, no more and no less, was all she was prepared to undertake.' This reminds us of the narrator-heroine of Margaret Atwood's *Surfacing* who strikes a symbolic retreat into the heart of the island forest to feel, "I lean against a tree. I am the tree leaning."

Although Carignano is apparently a barren place, it is precisely this barrenness that appeals to Nanda Kaul. Is it because of its resemblance to her own barren life? The reader is left to guess. The starkness of the Kasauli range, along with its rocks, and pines, its light and air, with its vast expanse and sweeping view towards the Northern peaks and the Southern plains pleases the old lady. At this stage of her life she seems to want nothing more. She, however, is not pleased with the scene in her garden, where the bird-mother feeds her nestlings. Their shrill screams seem maddening to her. Does it bring back unpleasant memories? She turns back to the opposite direction and walks to the topmost point of her garden. But even from here an unpleasant item dots the canvas,—the plodding postman.

The first chapter subtly introduces Nanda Kaul as a person as well as her present situation. Apparently, the lady has withdrawn from the plains, from friends and relatives, from all mundane superfluities of daily life, and also from her own past. She is determined to love her loneliness. We are also allowed a glimpse of her house as well as the view commanded from the spot, through Nanda Kaul's own point of view.

The very first chapter introduces the keynote of the novel, and simultaneously lets loose a number of ideas which will be gradually crystallized in course of the novel. But even at this stage it is quite evident that Anita Desai's primary interest is not the description of the landscape but the psychology of the protagonist and the landscape is used only to reflect symbolically the mindscape of Nanda Kaul. In the words of N.R. Gopal.

> In the very first chapter nature imagery has been used to portray the character of Nanda Kaul. She has had such a busy family life that in the evening of her life she wants to do nothing with family or society. She prefers her lonely isolated existence guarding her privacy fiercely and the news of Raka's arrival, conveyed to her through a letter, unsettles her. What she wanted was total withdrawal from society and hating human society so much so as to yearn to be a tree, a part of nature. In the authorial description in the Chapter I a parallel has been shown between her and a tree:

> She was grey, tall and thin and her silk saree made a sweeping, shivering sound and she fancied she could merge with the pine trees and be mistaken for one. To be a tree, no more and no less, was all she was prepared to undertake (1).
>
> But human beings cannot be trees howsoever they may yearn for it. This is the only novel of Anita Desai in which nature plays such a Antal role on the level of symbolism and imagery and it has to be accepted that she makes effective use of this technique to portray different characters. (Gopal 71)

Chapter 2

In the second chapter the history of the house, "Carignanc," is unfolded through the postman's silent reminiscing,—how it began as a colonial officer's family retreat, and then changed hands again and again until the colonials were flushed out after independence, and finally Nanda Kaul bought it.

The chapter, as it evokes and describes the colonial past of the Kasauli hill station as well as that of Carignano, superbly reflects the mild ironical touch which is usually associated with Austen or Forster. It also shows the author's awareness about the subaltern outsider's interest in, and amusement at, the inside drama of the big and high houses of the rich and the empowered. At the same time it also compresses in a nutshell an entire dimension of colonial history, the homesick colonial's search for a home away from home, which was simultaneously pathetic and absurd.

Chapter 3

With a few brush strokes, tinged with the flavour of an indulgent humour, the novelist describes the postman as he trudges up and meets Ram Lal, the servant-cum-cook at Carignano. The chapter is devoted to the commoners as they go about and follow the slow rhythmic life in this sleepy hill station, which has been finely captured even to the charming details like a truant school boy, or an easy-going whistling pony man, an officious postman and a quiet old servant sharing small talks as they trudge up the hillside.

The two come up together to find Nanda Kaul waiting at the gate in her typical erect posture. The postman hands over a letter to Nanda Kaul, who has already decided to refuse any request that the letter might possibly carry. What does this resolve suggest? Does this suggest that the old lady has parted ways from the past, or from human relationships and obligations? Is it really renunciation, or is it due to some deep-seated grievance or sense of wrong? Does this carry any clue to her retreat to the mountains at this age? We will get answers to these suspenseful questions in course of reading the novel.

Chapter 4

Chapter four focuses on Nanda Kaul's feelings after getting the letter. But in order to describe her reaction, the author first places her in her specific space, *i.e.,* a vantage point in the veranda, and allows us to get a glimpse and idea of the sights and sounds around. This is characteristic of Anita Desai's narrative style here. She would be continuously adjusting and re-adjusting our view of the heroine by relating the woman to the various points of the space around her, enveloping her, and also releasing her. We will discuss these aspects in detail when we shall examine the narrative technique of Anita Desai.

Nanda Kaul sits in the shaded cool veranda of Carignano in her accustomed posture in the old cane chair, with the letter on her lap. But instead of opening it she continues watching, absentmindedly, the birds as they are engaged in their little fightings or hunting. We become aware of the cicadas through her consciousness of the sound; of the pine trees as she listens to the sound of the pine-needles rubbing against the leaves, and smells their scent, or looks at the streaks of light reflected by the silvery needles. It is also through Nanda Kaul's eyes that we get a glimpse of the serene view of the hilltops across the valley with its church spires, schoolhouses and greenery. The loneliness and silence of the scene is accentuated by such small details including even a large butterfly which crosses over and distracts Nanda Kaul from her contemplation of the distant view.

It is, as it were, the flitting butterfly that brings her mind back to the letter lying unopened on her lap. The handwriting on the envelope shows that it is from her daughter Asha. The thought of Asha—the beautiful, complacent, shallow girl, dedicated to the single job of nurturing her hair and skin—also brings along in its train the thought of another contrasting figure; she is Tara, Asha's unhappy daughter. The failure of Tara's marriage has been summed up in a few sentences, as Nanda Kaul remembers her.

Tara, we come to know, has been reduced to a bundle of nerves, 'a helpless jelly' thanks to the ill-treatment from her husband. But Asha, blunt as she is, fails to understand why should Tara fail to be 'the successful diplomat's wife,' and pressurizes her to try again and again. In an earlier letter Asha had written to Nanda Kaul that since Tara's husband had been given a new posting in Geneva, she wanted Tara to accompany him and make another attempt at being 'happy'; the only problem was their little daughter Raka, who had been recovering from typhoid, but Asha was confident that this minor obstacle to 'happiness' could certainly be overcome.

At reading that letter Nanda Kaul felt so disgusted that she did not care to reply. And now she feels equally reluctant to open this follow-up message from Asha. However, when at last she opens the letter, it is to find the message that Raka, her great-grandchild, is already on her way to Kasauli.

Nanda Kaul feels both angry and disappointed,—angry because of her daughter's insensitive meddling into others' lives, and disappointed at this unwanted intrusion into her own space. Arrived at the fag end of her life, Nanda Kaul feels she wants only stillness and calmness; she only wants Carignano, and that little space—all to herself. But now an intrusion is thrust upon her, and it is imminent, she feels so dissatisfied that the perpetually soothing scenario around her fails to soothe her at this moment.

Chapter 5

Chapter five registers Nanda Kaul's reaction to the letter and her feeling of grievance. Significantly, during this hour of grievance Nanda Kaul does not look up at the snow-clad serene peaks, but instead gazes down the gorge towards the Punjab plains and silently argues with some absent addressee. Had she not done enough and suffered enough? Does not she have the right just to retreat into her 'nothingness?' The description of Nanda Kaul's aggrieved state of mind actually registers some of the basic concerns of feminist thinking regarding the woman's right to her own space, even if this space contains absolutely 'nothing.'

The chapter also gives a clue to Nanda Kaul's withering and decisive withdrawal as the veil over the past gets slightly ripped during this moment of grievance, and we are allowed a quick glimpse into the past when Nanda was a busy housewife. This past is not remembered by her as some shining vista; instead it seems to be like a gorge. The real gorge stretching in front of her, becomes metamorphosed, as it were, into an ugly choked gutter (an obviously cinematic technique too) on which crowds of heads,—heads of children, grandchildren, servants, guests surge up and clamour around her.

A scene from the past returns in a flash,—one day in the life of a housewife in her Vice-Chancellor husband's house in a small town in Punjab. This one day is symptomatic of all the other days when she had to be busy all the time with thankless and endless housework,—mending, sewing, supervising the cooking, issuing instructions to the servants, watching over the children in order to prevent accidents/injuries, receiving the husband's guests and streams of visitors, also bearing with their unashamed flattery. The compliments made her only angry. Was it because the compliments were paid to her just for 'a role,'—for competently playing a role that was thrust upon her, the role of the efficient, beautiful 'wife'—and not as an individual in her own right?

There is a momentary return from the crowded gaudy past to the contrastive present of grey senility. The contrast is finely suggested by the hint about her "knuckles." What was once splendid queenly beauty is now reduced to "two rows of yellow bones." Again she flits back to the past in her thought. But this brings no consolation of sweet memories. It is only the painful memories of many child-bearing, many confinements, endless child-rearing, along with all sorts of attendant annoyances, exhaustion, humiliation, and the compulsion of keeping up a posture in spite of all the exacting demands, since her husband wanted her to appear elegant before "his guests," never "hers."

As Nanda Kaul tries to remember the house, again the same feeling of un-belonging, and un-possession, comes back. It had been "his house, never hers," where she had only obeyed the calls of 'duty' like a slave. Who told her that all this was her duty? Who defined her 'duties,' or forced them upon her? The author suggests it was but self-imposed, and yet the self-imposition itself was conditioned by the patriarchal ideology that governed the society. This first journey of Nanda Kaul down memory lane helps us to understand her frustration and feeling of emptiness, the vacuity of un-fulfilment.

After coming to Kasauli Nanda Kaul had thought that at last she was released from the shackles of those endless 'duties.' Naturally she feels bitter that she should be forced against her wishes into the harness once more, compelled to accept once more the call for caring, comforting, communicating with another human.

Nanda Kaul feels she would have preferred to be an eagle freely gliding in the sky. But she knows she cannot be. Significantly at this moment it is a cuckoo—and not an eagle—that distracts her from the garden with a very soft, very musical 'domestic' tone. Here is a characteristic Anita Desai touch,—simultaneously ironical and evocative. So she surrenders with a sigh and goes to the kitchen to inform Ram Lal of the impending arrival.

The chapter further registers and brings under sharper focus Nanda Kaul's alienation as an abandoned, marginalized, and yet used and humiliated old woman.

The chapter in its facile flow of the narrative reveals some of the important aspects of Anita Desai's narrative technique. It is through Anita Desai's deft handling of the flashback technique that the past of Nanda Kaul with all her sufferings and humiliations, and the dichotomy between her appearance and the reality are brought into a dynamic relationship with the present. It also becomes increasingly clear that Anita Desai's primary interest is not the plot but the character—the 'flickerings of the innermost flame.' Actions are louder than words, and in the novel the feelings are demonstrated through actions and attitudes which assume symbolic significance. The gait of Nanda Kaul, her erect figure, her desire to be as free as an eagle, or to be as indifferent to the external world as a tree reveal the workings of her mind. Similarly, the ruggedness and barrenness of Carignano will also gradually assume symbolic significance and will further illuminate the character of Nanda Kaul.

We will discuss these aspects in detail in course of our discussion of Anita Desai's use of symbols and images as part of her narrative strategy for the embodiment of her vision in characters and situations. What cannot be stated can only be suggested, and it is here that symbols and images function as instruments for evoking the desirable suggestions. At this stage one should only keep his/her ears and eyes open to notice how the landscape, the various objects of nature, peculiarities of actions and behaviour, and verbal and physical expressions of feelings contribute to the development of the theme and the character of Nanda Kaul.

Chapter 6

Chapter six introduces Ila Das, Nanda Kaul's childhood friend. Initially, it is almost in a mocking tone that the poor woman is mentioned. Her "hideous voice" is likened to the crackling of suddenly awakened geese. But even though the shrill voice of Ila Das pains Nanda Kaul, she remembers with sympathy how this voice was Ila Das's 'tragedy' and how Ila Das has been all along blissfully unaware of this. She screeches into the telephone to tell Nanda Kaul that she has been posted in a village in the vicinity, and wants to meet Nanda. Nanda Kaul feels nervous about the possible impact of this meeting on her great-granddaughter, and tries to dissuade Ila Das against visiting her for the time being. But when she abruptly cuts the line Ila Das, in her innocent way, suspects nothing. She only wonders about the absolute lack of joy in Nanda Kaul's voice. This shows that in spite of her ridiculous appearance and ways Ila Das is basically innocent, well-meaning and sensitive as well.

The introduction of Ila Das is meant to present another section of the marginalized women. Unlike Nanda Kaul she is poor and a spinster, but it will be gradually revealed that in spite of the very many contrasts in their social positions, in their figures, and in their ways of living there is a basic affinity between the two. Apart from the fact that they are old friends, right from their school days, and know each other pretty well, both are also victims of a dominantly patriarchal society in their respective ways.

The sudden surfacing of Ila Das after so many years is a significant turning point of the plot. If the appearance of Ila Das marks 'the beginning of the end' she will also be instrumental in the 'end of the end' so far as Nanda Kaul's life is concerned. The telephone box or instrument of Nanda Kaul into which Ila Das screeches her presence will again play a momentous role when the news of her death will come through the same telephone and cause the death of Nanda Kaul. If in the first use of the telephone Nanda Kaul had cut the line now it is her life that is snapped. It should also be noted that telephone, which is a means of communication, reveals in both the cases enormous communication gaps.

Chapter 7

It is through a zigzag course between time present and time past as it flows through Nanda Kaul's consciousness, that the story is woven. In that sense it can also be called a memory-novel. Chapter seven opens in the midst of a hot midday at Carignano, when Nanda tries to rest by keeping her eyes tightly shut, and then shifts back to the past down memory lane. Lying on her bed in Carignano Nanda Kaul tries to remember another bed in another house where she used to practice this composure for years. In those days too she tried to shut out sound by shutting out light, and yet sounds, stealthy subdued ones, sneaked into her sleepless hours. Does this carry hint of the secret life of her husband that went on under her nose for years, a humiliation which she would have pretended to ignore and yet could not ignore altogether?

Again, those few moments of midday rest snatched off with a decision from others' demands, were her only personal time. As soon as the quota was spent family clamoured in, in the form of duties, responsibilities, concerns, and what not; she would have to stand patiently at the fixed centre of this swirling whirlpool.

These memories do not soothe her. She tries to locate some moment of peace in all those days, months, years each of which was exactly like another. Then suddenly she seems to recall one cool, silent evening by an abandoned badminton court. The games were over; people had left, and she was walking alone by the deserted court until she heard the car coming back. The owner had been out to drop 'one' of the guests home. She did not move. She stood there completely silent, completely alone, and watched him crossing the veranda to reach his small bedroom where Nanda Kaul had put him up. Is it a way of protest? She 'relished' the sensation of being alone. She remembers this lonely twilight as 'a moment of private triumph, cold and proud.' The touch of coolness brings her back to the present, to the Carignano afternoon.

The crowded memories, suddenly let loose—first by the letter from her daughter and then by the telephonic call from Ila Das, provide the long shot where suddenly, and almost inevitably the spotlight falls on the badminton court, a site associated with conjugal deceit.

Chapter 8

After tea Nanda Kaul continues to sit on the veranda in the late afternoon shade, and goes on reading a book about the house of 'a woman who lives alone.' She enjoys the book like chilled wine. Before her the hills are taking on the most beautiful water colour shades. She looks back at her own garden whose very bareness pleases her. Again this garden and house recede from her concern to usher in another house and another garden on the mental screen. It is a contrastive picture. The old house was a "full" crowded house, where she had to be at the centre of a busy world. And the garden too contained 'too many' trees with 'too many' parrots, whereas inside the house there were 'too many' servants, 'too many' guests coming and going, 'many' rooms and corners of the house always full of extra beds. She did not enjoy it; the lack of privacy vexed her. She felt tired with all the fuss and noise, work and more work,—with 'too many' trays of tea to be made and sent to this and that room, 'too many' meals, 'too many' dishes on the table, 'too much' to wash after every meal; also 'so many' children attending, 'so many' different schools and colleges, 'so many' tutors to coach them. The repetition of the phrase 'too many' and the word 'many' subtly evokes the claustrophobic life of the lady of this big house who lacked any space/time/leisure of her own. Now she can see 'she had suffered' from this excess. She decides that she has been glad to leave it all behind. She is also afraid that Raka's arrival may again put her back on that Sisyphean track of caring.

To her mind Raka appears as a veritable menace to her solitude and serenity. This is proleptic, because eventually Raka will not only disturb her placidity, but will also draw out the latent contradictions in her character—the conflict between her desire for withdrawal and her involvement in spite of herself—and ultimately put the mountain on fire, both literally and figuratively.

Chapter 9

Nanda Kaul knows now that all her life has been spent or wasted caring for others, and now she has lost the motivation. In this house, at last a house of her own, she just wants to revel in her freedom from obligations. Now she finds a projection of her own condition in the bare, empty garden of this house. So she does not want to change it or plant any new thing in it just as she does not want to add anything to her shrunk, pared, but 'radiantly single life' at this stage. Like her the garden also seems to have aged and withered till it has reached an 'elegant perfection.' She just cannot imagine a child in this garden. The very thought seems sickening to her.

Though Nanda Kaul feels distressed and agitated, it appears that even now she cannot disown responsibility. She goes over to the kitchen to inform Ram Lal about the child's imminent arrival and stay in Carignano. But it is ironical that she feels nervous and inadequate for the occasion. Once she had hosted big dinner parties with brilliant success, but now she does not seem to remember a single item with which to entertain a small child.

Ram Lal, himself unsure about the same, however, has his own diagnosis for the situation; it is old age. As in the previous chapters, in this chapter also Anita Desai follows the same narrative technique of flashback and interior monologues, and profuse use of powerful symbols, presented through the consciousness of Nanda Kaul. About her attitude to the garden, for example, the author says: "Unlike any other owner of the house and the garden she had not said: Here I will plant a willow, there I will pull out the Spanish broom and put in pompous grass instead. No, she reveled in its barrenness, its emptiness" (31). Very subtly but very surely Anita Desai calls our attention to the affinity between Nanda Kaul and the garden. The garden is as barren and as empty as she is. The garden thus becomes an 'objective correlative' for the feelings of Nanda Kaul after she has lived her life only to realize, rather late in the day, that it has all been barren and empty. Lest the reader misses the point Anita Desai makes it abundantly clear through her remarks:

> She no more wished to add to them than she wished to add to her own pared, reduced and radiantly single life. (31)

The chapter also introduces Ram Lal, an old servant of the household who has obviously seen better times in the hill station with richer and more sociable employers. But it is also obvious that the cultural level of Ram Lal is such that it is beyond his capacity to understand the mental condition of Nanda Kaul or her sense of barrenness. Now that Raka is coming, like an old obedient servant he wants to take instructions from Nanda Kaul about what to cook or how to entertain the new young guest. Nanda Kaul's pleadings of ignorance—"I don't know, Ram Lal, I don't know"—reveals the profound pathos of her life, and Desai's remark,—"she sighed, and suddenly clutched the edge of the table"—shows her struggle with herself in coming to terms with the unexpected development that has suddenly put her out of gear. Ram Lal, a man of obtuse sensibility does not understand it and in a fit of inspiration, as it were, hits upon a solution which he considers to be the best possible solution at the moment: "Potato chips [...]. All children like potato chips" (32).

The chapter presents Ram Lal who belongs to the fast vanishing tribe of loyal servants—a legacy of the feudal system of the colonial days—and he acts as a kind of foil to the highly sensitive nature of Nanda Kaul. But it must be said to the credit of Anita Desai that with a few powerful strokes of her brush she has been able to infuse life into the character of Ram Lal who appears as a familiar figure.

Chapter 10

In Chapter ten, the last chapter of Part One, we find that the caring self of Nanda Kaul which had been kept at bay with decision for years is now set for staging a comeback. Nanda Kaul is getting ready to receive her great grandchild. She would have gone to the taxi-stand herself but for the prying eyes of curious neighbours. So she sends Ram Lal instead to bring the child home. But during these last few hours of her privacy and her exclusive space she shows an ambivalence in her acts and feelings. On the one hand she would go into the guest room again and again to see if everything was alright; she adds small touches here and there, and even thinks of some fresh flowers by the bedside, when she bumps against the bed-post and receives a small injury on the leg. While nursing her bruise, Nanda Kaul tries hard to remember Raka, at least something, some small detail if possible. But among the crowd of her children and grandchildren she fails to spot this girl, though she remembers Raka's mother, Tara, perhaps because Tara's unhappiness and suffering stir her sympathy. But all the small details about so many children of different generations get mixed up in the twilight zone of memory. She cannot recall the time or place of Raka's birth, nor the particular gift she had sent to this particular baby, because she had sent so many various gifts to so many various babies of so many different mothers in their times. Howsoever she may try to on vision Raka's appearance she can conjure up no distinct image. This very attempt—to remember and identify—nevertheless shows that Nanda Kaul has, in spite of herself, started caring once again.

Simultaneously, on the other hand, Nanda Kaul feels annoyed and miserable that she will now have to deal with an individual who will moreover be dependent on her; that she will have to take care about her food, watch over her safety, worry over her fears and anxieties, devise ways of entertaining her. After bringing up so many children now she feels at a loss since she has forgotten all those devices she had been so adept in once for entertaining children. She also feels upset at the thought that, with another person, sleeping, playing, or going about in the house, she will have no privacy, no free space or moment for herself. All these years in Kasauli she has avoided every neighbour and relative, every connection with the past or present, excepting Ila Das, who had herself found her out and followed her to this sleepy hollow.

The author has finely captured the ambivalence of Nanda Kaul's approach at this juncture. The chapter closes with a fine evocative touch. As Nanda Kaul comes out to the veranda and waits for Raka to arrive, the pine-needles at the gate are still ruffled by the wind while glistening silvery in the sunlight; there is also a small cuckoo singing in the chestnut tree down the road, and the song sends a Tow, domestic call.' It seems to be a subtle and evocative hint to suggest that although Nanda Kaul has been likened to the charred pine trees by the gate, and she herself would have wanted to be a pine tree or an eagle, still she can also hear the Tow, domestic call' of the cuckoo.

In this chapter also Anita Desai gives some fine touches to give an idea of the disturbed state of the mind of Nanda Kaul. Nanda Kaul bumping her leg against the bed-post and getting a 'rainbow-tinted bruise' is one such touch. Her conflict is also indicated in her ambivalent attitude to Raka, whether she should try to make Raka comfortable by taking her to the club and by calling other children to play with her, or she should hold on to her aloofness, 'jealous of this privacy achieved only at the very end of her life' (36). The ruffled pine needles reflect the ruffled state of Nanda Kaul's mind. The cuckoo singing 'in the chestnut tree down by the road, with its low, domestic call,' prepares us for the arrival of Raka who is likely to force Nanda Kaul back to domesticity in a way.

PART II

If Part One has Nanda as its focus, Part Two focuses on Raka, as is also indicated by its sub-title, 'Raka Comes to Carignano.'

Chapter 1

'Raka' means moon. But Nanda Kaul perceives there is nothing moon-like about Raka. She is neither healthy nor calm or beaming in appearance. Rather the emaciated girl, the 'stranger' in Nanda Kaul's garden, looks more like a frightened thin insect which is unsure about itself. Henceforth the insect analogy will be repeatedly used for describing Raka. We shall take it up in greater detail in course of our discussion of Desai's use of images in the novel. However, for the time being we hear the sounds of the place through Raka's consciousness. Raka finds it to be a novel experience; she 'thinks' she has never before heard this voice of silence. Silently she watches around and takes note of the features of the house and the place. The child and the lady, both thin and bony, one due to illness and the other due to age, meet in a quick, almost reluctant, embrace. To the child's perception the old lady, tall and grey in silk, appears also like another pine among pine trees, whereas Nanda Kaul looks upon her as a 'mosquito flown up from the plains to tease and worry' her. Nanda Kaul only feels resentfully that Raka has come as an intruder whose presence would be teasing and worrying for her. However, she receives her as a matter of course, and casually leads her into the house.

The focus in the chapter, as has already been suggested, is on Raka, and Anita Desai takes particular care to suggest the affinities and differences between the host and the guest. However, the general focus is on the disturbed state of Nanda Kaul's mind on account of the external world, the world she has deliberately left behind, again intruding into her life in the form of Raka. The device of using functional images is continued as part of the narrative technique.

Furthermore with the arrival of Raka, a 'foreign element', there is an addition of a new structural element in the plot; we have been given enough hint that Raka cannot be domesticated. She is not meant to be a typical nice little girl whom everybody would like to love and caress.

Chapter 2

As Raka explores the place bit by bit we also come to know her, the peculiarities of her nature and ways bit by bit. Raka walks about her room in bare feet like some newly caged animal. Apparently she is not the typical pampered or sociable child. She meets a spider and a lizard, and is not scared. She is less interested in flowers than in a discarded snail's shell. She moves about stealthily, and speaks almost nothing. Silently and stealthily she begins to explore the nooks and corners of the house. Eventually she will explore the whole place. Whereas Nanda Kaul rarely leaves Carignano, Raka, on her very first day here, comes out—that too through the backyard—and makes a survey of the area, spots a club, a factory, some huge vultures and distant hills like gleaming pebbles on golden hilltops. Then, like a child, she gets absorbed in search of a cricket and spends the entire afternoon in the mission.

The chapter brings to light the essential nature of Raka, her love of the external nature, her desire to scan the landscape in minutest details and her distaste for staying indoors. All these aspects of her character are presented through her actions and behaviour. The use of functional imagery is evident in the references to various insects and creatures and the juxtaposition of contrastive images like small cicadas and 'huge vultures.'

One interesting aspect of this chapter is the sudden glimpse of the sleeping Ram Lal that we are given through the eyes of Raka: "Ram Lal lay on his string cot, his limbs flung out to its four corners, his cap on his nose, lifting and falling with the low growls and sudden snores that came and went beneath it" (42). The picture shows Desai's keen observation that enables her to capture realistically and convincingly the image of a sleeping servant enjoying his after-lunch siesta.

Chapter 3

As Ram Lal gets busy with preparation for afternoon tea Raka slides down the knoll in search of Pasteur Institute. Just a little while ago Ram Lal had told her about the factory including imaginary and real gory details about the preparation of serums for injection. Raka is fascinated by the macabre element in Ram Lal's narration about mad dogs, mad jackals, the animals killed for getting the serum, and even the ghosts of people killed by dogs or snakes in the hills, who are supposed to haunt the hillsides. Raka feels excited and wants to set out for the ravine at once. Nanda Kaul does not guess the reason but can feel the child's restiveness, and encourages her to take a walk out. She wants not to get involved, not to be drawn into a child's world once again: "Let her contain or release herself whatever she could do best, thought Nanda Kaul drinking the bitter dregs" (45). The 'bitter dregs' which literally refers to the last dregs of the tea she had been drinking it also refers metaphorically to the last dregs of her life which has become bitter on account of her renewed encounter with the social life through Raka.

The chapter is also important in registering the growth of relationship between Raka and Ram Lal who tells the child, in his innocent way, not only about the factories and houses but also about ghosts of people who have died of dog-bite and snake-bite and who now wander about on the hillsides. The stories of Ram Lal also throw light on his character who, as a simple rustic person, genuinely believes that people dying of snake-bite or dog-bite really turn into ghosts.

Furthermore, it should also be noted how the communication gap between Nanda Kaul and Raka is suggested when, to her great grandmother's question, 'Didn't you rest at all?,' she does not care to reply. Will the gap gradually widen and become unbridgeable at the end or will it close?

Chapter 4

In this chapter Raka is seen through Nanda Raul's eyes. Raka is so withdrawn and silent that Nanda Kaul cannot make out what the child thinks or does. She just seems to disappear for hours. Sometimes she can spot her scrambling up a stony incline, or wandering down a lane, but always alone. She is careless about her appearance or the small bruises or cuts she incurs in course of her small lonely adventures on the hills. She wanders about with thoughtful eyes and still look as if she has been to strange wonderlands.

Although it is not Nanda Kaul's policy to question, nevertheless she feels annoyed that she should be thus forced to worry about others again. Is there no respite for her, she would ask in silent resentment. However, when she writes to Asha, she takes care not to express any of the resentment she feels so keenly. This only shows her innate dignity. She just informs Asha about the safe arrival of her granddaughter. She also thinks that she would convey the message to Raka that she did not want to interfere into her ways. Nanda Kaul has already felt that the child is a perceptive one and would understand the message.

However, Nanda Kaul's ambivalence is apparent in her mixed response to the child's behaviour. Whereas the latter's presence irks Nanda Kaul, her long absences perturb her. Her calm is ruffled by the child's unpredictable disappearances and reappearances. She also feels bad that her peace should be so disturbed by another human.

But Raka seems to be simply beyond her control and blissfully indifferent to her feelings. When she looks reproachfully at the child on her return after a long bout of absence, the child calmly and effortlessly ignores her. Whereas the old lady has to 'decide' whether to ignore or 'reject' the child, the child 'rejects' her automatically.

Day-by-day Nanda Kaul realizes that without any effort Raka has been what Nanda Kaul herself would have liked to be, but failed in being. She admits to herself that Raka was not like any other child in the family. She seemed to have no needs; she made no demands. Like herself the child resembled more an insect on the hillsides than a human. She also realizes that both of them wanted the same thing—to be left alone to pursue an intensely individual reclusive life amongst the rocks and trees of the mountain.

At the same time Nanda Kaul also understands the basic difference between herself and Raka: for herself, the desire for reclusion was a kind of willful reaction to the maltreatment of life, but for the child it was just automatic, natural, spontaneous, effortless, something in-born. She was, as it were, born to it. As Nanda Kaul watches the child gliding down the hills towards the ravines she feels the stirring of a new feeling in her, a kind of admiration for the child.

It appears that Raka has been making a dent into Nanda Kaul's consciousness; her facade of indifference and aloofness has already been under attack and getting undermined in consequence.

The chapter thus, while highlighting the differences between Nanda Kaul and Raka, and Nanda Kaul's realization that 'she was not part of Nanda Kaul's life,' also gives another dimension to Nanda Kaul's character as she realizes that Raka 'was the finished, perfected model of what Nanda Kaul herself was merely a brave, flawed experiment' (47).

Chapter 5

In the meantime Raka drops lower and lower until she reaches the backyard of the serum factory. It is strange that the child should be drawn by this shabby dumping ground of the factory covered with rubbish and factory waste. Once she also sees a whole snake which she watches in a trance of fascination and fear. She approaches closer to the factory where the air smells of cinder, serum, chloroform and animal residues. She also imagines that she can smell the dogs' boiled brains, and the caged rabbits' fear (about which Ram Lal had told her bizarre stories).

It may be noted that Raka does not gaze up toward the snowy peaks, but instead she gazes down at the plains, which are smothered by dust, excepting the Chandigarh lake, which appeals to her imagination like a "snake's eye." Anita Desai's description of Raka's various memories of snakes—'the tips of snakes' tail parting the cracks of rocks,' 'slit eyes watching her from grottoes of shade,' 'the slither of scales upon the ground'—show her keen observation of the behaviour of snakes and her ability to use it for a realistic portrayal of the psychology of a child.

On her way back Raka disturbs the crickets and they raise an alarm in chorus. By a slight mistake Raka lands at the club which is deserted at this hour, and then dashes across towards Carignano. Later in the story she will come to the club again, that time too in anonymity.

Chapter 6

By the time Raka reaches home Ram Lal has been already arranging for her bath and waiting for her to return. As Raka tumbles down the knoll with grass and thorn sticking to her hair and sandal, she looks like a bird fallen out of its nest which has again fallen out of the tree. This is metaphorical as well, since Raka is indeed the lost child from a broken home. *Fire on the Mountain* is the one novel of Anita Desai which abounds in such beautiful and eloquent images.

Raka has some friendly conversation with Ram Lal on the subject of snakes and jackals. Ram Lal has very well-defined and wiry ideas about all sorts of creatures, including ghosts which are absorbed by Raka. But now Ram Lal makes a suggestion which cannot have much appeal for Raka; that she should go to the club instead of looking for jackals in the ravines which is not safe for a child by any means. Ram Lal nostalgically recalls better days with richer masters, and tells Raka about the club-life in those prime times of the past. Obviously this was a colonial past which has been evoked in this novel in various contexts.

Even before Raka can start her bath the dust storm bursts in. And there follows a vivid powerful description of the storm. This is one of the many purple patches of *Fire on the Mountain,* which account for the special flavour of the book.

Ram Lal is worried lest the storm knocks over his 'hamam.' But Raka is excited at the prospect of a fire wildly spreading through the garden and the hill as well.

Soon the storm is over. The blinding dust and the roaring wind subside, leaving the scene cool and clear. Again, with a fine stroke the author brings out this restoration. During the storm the birds had hidden in whatever shelter they could find. Now 'dizzy parrots, in a phosphorescent flock, burst out of the pines and spurted away, leaving their shrieks behind.' Gay relief is the mood all-around, from Ram Lal filling the bucket, or Raka skipping behind him like a 'pet insect', to the cuckoo calling on the knoll. However, it is hard to tell if the mood bypasses Nanda Kaul; because as Nanda Kaul looks at them from her window—crossing the yard towards the 'hamam'—her suppressed annoyance is brought out by a small movement, slapping at a pair of bumbling flies on the window-pane.

The main interest of the chapter lies in further delineating the character of Raka through her conversations with Ram Lal, and in the process we also get further picture of Ram Lal whose character also gets highlighted in the process. One should also note the use of animal imagery and nature imagery in the chapter, which has been elaborately woven around a carefully patterned structure of images and symbols.

Chapter 7

It has become Raka's habit to steal out after tea in the afternoon. But today as she is about to slip away unnoticed, Nanda Kaul too quickly gets up and offers to come with the child 'for a walk.' Raka's dismay is obvious. This is the hour when she would search for ripe berries in the bush. Nanda Kaul, who had reared so many kids has now forgotten the eating habit of children,—that they should require something to munch between meals; and Raka is too shy to ask for anything. So the old lady's whim is unwelcome to her. Furthermore, she has no craving for companionship and prefers to wander alone as the lonely cloud. So she is vexed at this sudden development. She is also apprehensive that a 'walk' might mean for the old lady just a stroll through the market or a brief visit to the club, both of which are unpalatable to her.

To her surprise Nanda Kaul comes out in her walking shoes, swinging a walking stick and asks pleasantly if they should go to the Monkey Point. The awkward pair stiffly walk side-by-side as the subdued afternoon descends on the bare hills. Even if Nanda Kaul feels the exercise a bit trying she won't let anybody guess. She would lift her stick as if only to indicate to Raka this and that point of interest. One such point is the hill top with the ruins of a burnt house. Nanda Kaul tells Raka the story of that fire which not only ruined the house but also left its lonely dweller, an old lady, mad. Nanda Kaul wonders if the old lady would not have preferred to die there in the fire instead of being taken away somewhere else from this resort. Does this carry a proleptic hint about the oncoming final fire which is not too far away.

Nanda Kaul also tells Raka about the hidden life in this dead house,—how one shower of rain will bring out hundreds of flowers out of the dry stone, flowers which the old lady had planted once. Here is again a fine touch to suggest that the emotions, the soft feelings have not altogether died down in Nanda Kaul's heart. Perhaps these, withered or suppressed as they are, may be just waiting for a 'shower of rain' and they will blossom again. Though initially Nanda Kaul was so very much against the prospect of having anybody in the house, it is apparent that within days of Raka's arrival Nanda Kaul's hard resistance has started to soften, to melt.

Nanda Kaul disapproves of the changes towards mundane improvisations that seem to have joined the obtrusive tourists to ruin the beauty and peace of the place. She nostalgically remembers her early years here when the place was like a 'haven,' and cites Hopkins's poem 'Heaven Haven.' We get an unexpected glimpse of a delightful side of Nanda Kaul, her fine imaginative sensibility. As she asserts, 'it seemed to apply' to her personal context, it also reveals a courageous effort to make peace with life, to accept the compulsive withdrawal as a kind of blessed peace. This shows a degree of inner strength and profundity which makes for Nanda Kaul's elegance.

At this point suddenly she laughs aloud. This is the first time since the beginning of the novel that we hear her laugh this way. The immediate cause of this outburst is the funny behaviour of a horde of wild *langurs.* Both the old lady and the child enjoy the refreshing laughter. Then, as they go downhill, Nanda Kaul points out to Raka an old house which is used as the summer holiday home for Delhi school children. She pictures the happiness of the children holidaying there, and then broaches the tentative suggestion if Raka would like to go to a school in Kasauli, say as a boarder at Sanawar. But Raka is shocked at the suggestion. All sorts of routine, discipline, or order are hateful to her. She feels so resentful that in her sullenness she quickens her pace and outstrips Nanda Kaul by running downhill. The old lady catches up with some effort. At the same time she too feels baffled at the child's unforeseen reaction to her offer. Actually she had meant it to be an offer to the child, an invitation to stay with her always and ever, to make Kasauli her home. But Raka's visible shock at the suggestion of her being sent to school and a boarding house only shows how averse she is to any idea of discipline. She must remain free, as free as an insect, untamed and undisciplined. The chapter also shows the change in Nanda Kaul's attitude to Raka, and her growing involvement in her life. She came out of her groove to make the offer of sending Raka to school, so that the child could have stayed on at Kasauli, but Raka misses the point.

Chapter 8

Nanda Kaul and Raka reach Monkey Point. Nanda Kaul sits down on the bench at the foot; she is tired and too old for the climb. So Raka goes up while Nanda Kaul waits for her at the bottom. Nanda Kaul is both alarmed and impressed at the way Raka goes up as if in no time.

Once up there, Raka also feels happy. Although originally she had planned to come here all by herself, and although Nanda Kaul's reference to the Sanawar school made her feel bad, now after coming up here and standing under the open sky, amidst the chaotic wind, her resentment is blown away. In every direction all-around a vast sweeping canvas is spread to the infinite horizon, and the countless hills, wave upon wave, of varied colours create the illusion of a sea. The roaring wind through the pines also evokes the roaring sound of sea waves. Raka is keenly delighted imagining herself as a shipwrecked crew, clinging to his boat, a rock in her case. She even sings out happily: 'alone in my boat on the sea.'

It is already dark at the foot of the hills when Raka comes down. Nanda Kaul agitatedly springs from her seat to meet Raka halfway, and on finding her safe and intact feels relieved. Why this 'agitation?' Does this suggest that Nanda Kaul has already become involved once again? Or, perhaps she had never really become detached, but only had tried to persuade herself that she did not care any more for anything or anybody?

Anyway, 'they walked home in a great silence,' a silence that eloquently suggests the awkward gap separating these two persons. When they reach home Raka, who had remained silent in the company of her great grandmother, shouts out, on seeing Ram Lal, 'What's for dinner?,' and runs forward. Is it as much running to Ram Lal as it is running away from Nanda Kaul?

Chapter 9

After the one excursion to the Monkey Point Nanda Kaul, however, does not repeat it. Instead she would open one of the books by the tea-table when Raka furtively slips off the veranda and takes her accustomed route among rocks and bushes, rubbish and chutes, while carefully avoiding the Mall and its people. Nanda Kaul watches her from a distance. She does not want to impose herself on Raka. But at the same time she cannot remain completely indifferent.

One evening at tea she tentatively suggests to Raka about going down to the club sometimes. From her past experiences at 'socialising' which had invariably failed, Raka has developed no interest in club life as such. Subsequently her prolonged illness had left her more unsocial and dreamy. She tries to parry the suggestion about the club by mildly retorting that her Nani too does not go to the club. Nanda Kaul is astonished at this reply from the child and then happily reaches out to this great-granddaughter who seems to resemble her so much. She exclaims in surprised delight: 'You are exactly like me, Raka.'

But Raka feels embarrassed at this outburst of emotion. And Nanda Kaul is also sensitive enough not to feel her reaction. Both fall silent and watch the birds in the garden. Raka takes the excuse that the birds cannot feed their chicks so long as Raka and her nani are there, and runs for her 'evening walk.' An element of disdain drips from Nanda Kaul's disconsolate voice. The chapter further develops the relationship between Nanda Kaul and her great grandchild, and foregrounds their semblance in spite of apparent incompatibility. However, while Nanda Kaul gradually, though rather reluctantly, concedes to get involved in the affair of Raka, the child would have nothing of it.

Chapter 10

At last Raka goes to the club, but not in the afternoon when jolly children use to throng there. She sneaks into the big summer party in the darkness of night. She had heard from Ram Lal about the party, obviously along with Ram Lal's own fond additions and exaggerations, as well as his comparisons between the glorious days of the past and the drab ways of the present in the hill station social life.

When the drums start at night Raka climbs out of her window and quietly ventures out into the thick darkness of Kasauli. Once entering the club she sees bright light and young men playing billiard. She feels scared of them, more scared than the jackals or nightjars can make her. She prefers darkness and walks under the windows. Across the garden, she spots the ball room about which Ram Lal had told her. Desperately she dashes through the garden though nobody seems to notice her. On reaching the veranda outside the ball room she hides in a dusty corner, and peeps through the thick dusty curtain to watch the revelry inside.

Chapter 11

But the scene inside proves to be a great shock to Raka. Where were the kings, queens and rosy court of Ram Lal's story? There were only madmen and rioters making wild gestures to the loud band. The scene, which appears to her childish mind as nothing but rampant lunacy, leaves her shattered. She wants to close her eyes and wish it away as some nightmare. People had dressed up as various animals and were mimicking the animal movements, while laughing, drinking, singing, and dancing. But the child cannot follow this adult game. She is scared like anything and flees the place crying. The club scene has called up in her mind another memory, her father coming home drunk from a party, abusing her mother while she lay paralysed in fear. Her mother's cry becomes mingled into the jackal's cry in the ravine outside. Somehow she manages to run back to Carignano, to her own room, silent dark quiet.

Chapter 12

It takes the child a few days to get over the trauma. During this period she seems to lose her normal springing movement and restiveness of an insect, and becomes still as a twig. Then she resumes her usual wanderings. As she glides down the hills Nanda Kaul 'surreptitiously' watches her,— first from the window, then from the railing. The question is why 'surreptitiously?' Nanda Kaul can sense a change; she can feel the hidden tension in the child's bearing. But she cannot guess the cause. Nor does she want her to know about her worry. She also cannot understand the child's fascination for the Pasteur Institute, which, to her, was only ugly and spoilt the view, while adding to the heat.

Raka returns home in the late evening, playing with a chestnut and muttering under her breath, 'I don't care—I don't care—I don't care for *anything.*' Nanda Kaul had similar feelings at the beginning of this story; but can she claim the same attitude now? Perhaps not. Nanda Kaul, who had been strolling up and down in her garden (is it anxiety?) sees her, takes note of the dust in her hair, the scratch on her knees, but asks nothing. Instead she suggests a pony ride which Raka at once dismisses on the ground that the pony man will always be there, and therefore it will be no fun. Nanda Kaul understands and agrees to her point.

At this moment Raka catches the glimpse of a sudden glow on the eastside hills. She thinks it is the full moon. Nanda Kaul knows better; it is a big forest fire, which is common at this time of the year. This is Raka's first experience of a forest fire, and although it is far away she is excited and stands in a trance.

Throughout the night Raka keeps getting out of bed and stealing into the drawing room to look at the fire spreading in the distance. She seems to have become obsessed with the fire. Her wakefulness keeps Nanda Kaul awake in her room. Eventually the child, worn out by fatigue, falls asleep on the drawing room sofa where she is discovered by Ram Lal in the morning.

The reference to the forest fire which fascinates Raka in this chapter is proleptic, as it is Raka who will finally put the entire hillside on fire. At this point the distant fire is 'like a dream—silent, swift and threatening.' It is like a fire in a dream, because 'they could neither smell the burning pine trees nor hear the crackling and hissing.'

Here is an instance of the fine masterly touch by means of which Anita Desai would prepare the reader for a forthcoming occasion, when the reader would recognize its connection with an earlier event and would thus be able to respond to the way the author constructs her thematic and artistic significances.

Chapter 13

Raka has found a confidante in Ram Lal. Together they have long conversations about stealthy excursions and ghosts of various brands. Looking at their cosy stance by the hamam in June afternoons Nanda Kaul realizes that Ram Lal can arouse Raka's interest and hold it which she cannot do. Does she feel a bit jealous?

Suddenly a band of langurs arrive with all the accompanying yelling and raving. But when Ram Lal picks up a stone to chase away a mother monkey with the kid hanging on to her belly, Raka passionately intervenes.

Nanda Kaul feels pained that Raka, who is so friendly with Ram Lal, did not even call her 'nani' to come out and have a look at the monkeys. This pain is another symptom of the growing involvement on her part, revealing a basic ambivalence in her approach.

Chapter 14

A letter comes from Asha with the information that Tara, Raka's mother, had another breakdown and had to be admitted in a nursing-home. Nanda Kaul decides against sharing this information with Raka. Of course, she would like to save the child from unhappiness. At the same time she has also been nursing a wound: since Raka preferred to keep her secrets to herself why should she make all the concession. Again, she also feels more pity for the child who has to depend on her.

Raka, however, continues to be blissfully unaware of her dependence, and moves about as independent and solitary as ever. Nanda Kaul wonders if the child realizes at all how solitary she is. Nanda Kaul perceives with amazement how different Raka is from any other child she has ever seen, so different that solitude never bothers the child, she never wants attention. Nanda Kaul has to be 'stubbornly' alone, with a decision. Raka is naturally alone, without having to make any effort to be so. She even goes to bed alone. Though long habits prompt Nanda Kaul to go and tuck the child in comfortably, telling her a soothing story to send her to sleep, she stubbornly stays back. She reminds herself that she did not come to Carignano for this, for resuming such duties once again at the fag end of life.

As Raka sleeps in her room Nanda Kaul lies awake in the adjacent room, thinking of Raka,—how she came to Carignano uninvited and then settled down naturally, automatically, like some mouse or cricket. Nanda Kaul wonders if she should leave Carignano to Raka; because, among all her acquaintances and relatives Raka alone seems to understand the place.

At this point a student of English literature is reminded of an obvious comparison. It is the thought of Ruth Wilcox in E.M. Forster's *Howard's End.* Prior to her death, Ruth Wilcox, an elderly British lady, had wanted to leave her country house, called 'Howard's End' to Margaret Schlegel, a young friend of hers, because Ruth Wilcox had felt that Margaret alone could understand the spirit of the place, and therefore she should be the only true inheritor. Of course her legal survivors,— her husband and children—did not obey her will since Margaret was no blood relation; but ultimately she got it nevertheless, because the house 'chose' its own inheritor.

Anyway, that is another story. And Carignano has no been envisioned by the author or her protagonist as a place with 'a spirit of its own' like Forster's 'Howard's End.' And for Nanda Kaul, making a will means too much of an effort, what with inviting the lawyer, seeing people, etc.,—a botheration she never wanted. But she now knows one thing clearly; that she does not want Raka to go away from her or from the place any more.

The most significant aspect of this chapter is Nanda Kaul's realization that Raka naturally belongs to this place and her recognition of her own desire to bequeath the house to her.

Obviously Nanda Kaul has come far away from her initial 'rejection' of Raka whom she had considered only an intruder into her privacy, solitude and freedom. Nanda Kaul had come to Carignano 'to be alone. Stubbornly to be alone,' and now 'She wished no one to go either—certainly not Raka.'

Chapter 15

Rain sets in following high wind in the mountains. Here is an instance of Desai's superb description,—terse, arresting, evocative, and relevant—as she captures in printed words the devastating wind and the intense downpour that chases the storm.

Along with the rain a new element enters the narration. It is the narration-within-narration. It marks the beginning of Nanda Kaul's story-telling sessions. While watching the rain, both the old lady and the child feel a kind of restlessness, a 'release.' While Raka strokes a little bronze Buddha on the tabletop, Nanda Kaul suddenly begins her story. It begins casually, with the 'information' that the Buddha had been brought from Tibet by Nanda Kaul's father. Raka, who is normally very selective in listening is now surprised and interested.

Having started the story once, there is no stopping for Nanda Kaul. She goes on adding up beautiful, impressive and fantastic details one after another. The author leaves some fine hints regarding the authenticity of these autobiographical reminiscences. For example, Nanda Kaul's voice rises 'unnaturally' as she tells about her explorer father's wonderful and extraordinary adventures and experiences, his many collections from which, of course, only the Buddha remains with her. We will learn much later, almost near the end of the novel that the little Buddha had been bought from a traveling pedlar.

The chapter presents a new dimension of Nanda Kaul's character; her deliberate concoction of stories, her myth-making. On the one hand it is a kind of wishfulfilment, and on the other hand, it is a defensive mechanism so necessary for the maintenance of her self-respect. Although she begins to tell the stories to captivate the attention of Raka she knows that it is all lie, a big lie that characterizes her life.

Chapter 16

As the rain continues, Nanda Kaul too continues her spinning. She switches from stories about her father to stories about her husband, 'raising' her voice above the rain and thunder. The story is now about the luxurious and exotic collection of her Vice-Chancellor husband, which are, again, not brought over to Carignano, since they were either given away to the next Vice-Chancellor or distributed among his large family. As she narrates, Nanda Kaul "covers" her eyes, as if she is "dazzled" by the splendour of her own fiction.

At this point Raka seems to lose interest. Nanda Kaul releases Raka and together they go out to look at the flowers, if they have come out with the rain. Then suddenly Nanda Kaul remembers something at which her voice betrays the tenor of 'a true remembrance'; it is about a small detail regarding Tara, Raka's mother, when she was a child. Tara used to enjoy the first burst of flowers after a rain, and used to sing in delight, 'Rainy days are lily days [...].'

Chapter 17

The following morning Raka comes to understand what her mother meant by the song. Pink flowers have suddenly burst out all over the hillside. They came out in the night after the first rain. Ram Lal fills the milk jug with some flowers and puts it on the breakfast table. Raka remembers what Nani said last night about her mother and wants to know if her mother used to come here frequently. Nanda Kaul cannot remember. In fact she has no distinct memory about the individual associations of her grandchildren. The only thing she remembers about Tara is her cry of delight at seeing the flowers.

Suddenly Raka asks if the letter that came some days ago was from her mother. Nanda Kaul has to tell her that it was from her grandmother and that her mother has been ill again, and at once she repents her own inability to tell comforting lies in spite of knowing the need of it. Here the author again leaves a hint about the element of fantasy and fiction in Nanda Kaul's 'reminiscences.' Nanda Kaul silently rebukes herself for telling the cruel truth to the child, since, she feels it is too hard to bear with naked truth, and must be especially hard for a child. Does this silent self-reproach offer a justification for, or, explanation of her fantasy-weaving?

Raka, however, does not show her reaction, excepting a pale face, a flatness in her voice and an expression of deliberate indifference. And Nanda thinks perhaps she can absorb the bad news since she has been accustomed to see her mother in sick bed so many times in her small life When Raka says she wants to go out Nanda Kaul feels relieved, though a bit disappointed as well.

The chapter further reveals Nanda Kaul's ambivalence in regard to Raka whom she has not yet been able to win over, as she regrets telling her the truth about her mother who is in a Nursing Home again. Then come—and this is very vital —her observations on fact and fantasy: "Fantasy and fairy tales had their place in life, she knew it too well. Why then did she tell the child the truth? Who wanted truth? Who could stand it? Nobody. Not even herself. So how could Raka?" One needs illusions to live by. But the world of fantasy, though created as a means of defensive mechanism, cannot last forever, and a time will come, by the end of the novel, when this world of fantasy will totally collapse and bring about the tragic end of Nanda Kaul.

Chapter 18

Chapter 18 gives an inner view of the working of Raka's mind. Raka springs out of the house and immediately heads for the burnt house on the hill. It is an abandoned place with blackened empty rooms, unhinged doors and windows, and sagging roof. Raka climbs over the broken stairs, and stands still listening to the silence as if she had been waiting for some catastrophic event. The scenes of devastation and failure, a ruined house and an unfinished one nearby, have a strange appeal for Raka. She feels irresistibly drawn towards such scenes.

Her own childhood places and associations have no such appeal for her. She was, as it were, an outsider in those nurseries and bedrooms of her infancy. In comparison she likes Carignano much better. Still it is an orderly place, clean and dry, and the orderliness seems constricting to her. On the other hand, the 'ravaged, destroyed, barren spaces' of Kasauli draw her. She is happy when she freely wanders about by the ravines, under the pines, or on the windy peaks.

Standing in the blackened frame of the burnt house which would be leveled any day, Raka imagines herself as if she were a pine tree in flames. Then she rushes out and runs down, alarming the hidden birds which start calling madly. The caretaker of the burnt house identifies the running child as 'the crazy one from Carignano.'

An important aspect of this chapter is a sly hint—a proleptic one again—about Raka's fascination for a scene of devastation: 'The hill with its one destroyed house and one unbuilt, on the ridge under the fire-singed pines, appealed to Raka with the strength of a strong sea-current-pulling-dragging. There was something about it—illegitimate, uncompromising and lawless—that made her tingle.' It is obvious that the adjectives— 'illegitimate, uncompromising and lawless' are eminently applicable to Raka as well. It is, therefore, natural that 'the scene of devastation and failure somehow drew her, inspired her.' Here lies the seed of the future act of her putting the mountain on fire.

Chapter 19

The spell of rain is over. The dust has returned. The pink flowers have disappeared. But Nanda Kaul cannot give up her story-telling. So she continues about her parental house in Kashmir, adding up extravagant and fantasizing details about the interior and exterior as well as about the life style of the inmates. As she spins the yarn of stories she speaks in an "unusually high-pitched voice" which makes Raka feel uneasy. It seems to have become a kind of compulsion on Nanda Kaul's part,—to hold Raka's attention. She seems unwilling to stop talking and thus let Raka out of her sight. She puts up picture after picture for the child's consumption, from a private zoo inside the house to free animals in the garden outside. She hurries on from item to item 'with an unaccustomed lightness and dreaminess of tone'. Apparently she cannot stop.

What does this change in Nanda Kaul—from indifference to involvement—indicate? Does this suggest any imminent disaster, or disintegration? Though Raka does not care to notice, the reader is given the hint about 'a storm of disintegration' crossing the old yellowed face. The enigma of this 'storm of disintegration' will be clear only towards the end of the novel when we shall realize how out of profound pathos and misery Nanda Kaul was obliged to lose her integrity. Or, is it after all a question of integrity or of some deeper necessity arising out of her predicament itself? Anyway, in spite of her 'stories' Raka feels impatient. She wants to be released. She seeks the chance to bolt out.

Chapter 20

Though Raka wants to go Nanda Kaul cannot let her go. Raka is bluntly unresponsive and even positively embarrassed by any attempt at endearments. Still Nanda Kaul would be impatiently waiting for the truant child, and as soon as she comes home she would start another fragment of a story. Incidentally, all the time she assumes that these are reminiscences of real things and events, and not fabricated fiction. This time she would start a narration about the pet animals in her husband's house. A cloud of skepticism has been gathering in Raka's eyes, but Nanda Kaul keeps her own eyes 'averted' so that the flow of her narration does not get halted.

Raka wants to be released from this intimacy which she finds 'disagreeable.' She longs for any excuse to run away from this 'fantasy world' of the old lady. She yawns in boredom and Nanda Kaul feels sad.

It is interesting to note that in the course of this chapter Raka feels 'disappointed' when what she had taken to be forest fire only turned out to be the effects of the moon. This disappointment is significant as Anita Desai uses it only to gradually prepare the reader for the final catastrophe.

Chapter 21

Raka has slipped out. But now Nanda Kaul has come to the stage when she misses her, longs for her company, and feels restive during the child's absence.

It is during one such afternoon that Ila Das calls on the telephone. It is decided after a long talk, to Nanda Kaul's consternation and boredom—that Ila Das will be coming to tea the next day.

Nanda Kaul waits for Raka who has not returned yet. Nanda Kaul wonders again if she should leave the house to Raka after all; because Raka was a wild creature, and like a wild creature, she did not need a house. Then should she leave it to Tara who perhaps will need a shelter some day! She cannot decide. She also thinks of clearing the house, leaving it bare and clean for Raka.

Significantly, she realizes how she has filled all the imaginary houses of the past with the furniture of imagination, but feels thankful to herself that she has not misused Carignano, she has not violated the sanctity of Carignano as it were. Let it be kept clear, even clear of herself, so that Raka can inherit it.

The chapter ends with a short paragraph of cryptic sentences: 'Clear the house. Clear it of Raka? No, not that. Of herself? Yes, soon, soon enough.' Coming events cast their shadows ahead. These suspenseful sentences foreshadow the imminent death of Nanda Kaul.

PART III

Whereas Part II has the subtitle, 'Raka Comes to Carignano,' the subtitle of Part III is 'Ila Das Leaves Carignano.' Ila Das comes to Carignano as well as leaves Carignano in this section, and indeed dominates the scene in this part of the narration.

Chapter 1

Nanda Kaul waits for Ila Das to arrive. Tea is already laid on the table. Then Ila Das appears at the end of the road, followed by wild school-boys, clamouring, insulting, teasing the old woman. The poor lady unfortunately invites this kind of attention by her appearance, her cracked voice, her broken umbrella. At last she is saved by Ram Lal from the persecuting cruelty; he chases away the boys who are still bubbling with delight in having such fun at the expense of an innocent creature. Her breathlessness reminds Ram Lal of the unpleasant analogy of 'an old animal that has been made to run before the hounds.'

This is the first glimpse we get of Ila Das, and this is symptomatic. Well-meaning Ila Das has been a target all along; she has been at the receiving end of life, and for no fault of her own. As it has already been suggested, both Ila Das and Nanda Kaul are victims of the dominantly patriarchal society though in different ways. It is also to be noted how the society treats a helpless old woman with all the cruelties at its command. Ila Das is a Welfare Officer but she will become the hapless victim of the cruel society which is not interested in actual welfare but in sticking to traditional norms of the society howsoever unfair and inhuman these may be. Her sincere efforts to prevent a child marriage will bring about her terrible end when she will be mercilessly raped and murdered.

Chapter 2

Ila Das is accustomed to persecution by jeering mobs all her life. Nanda Kaul wonders, if Ila had not drawn such derisive attention even as a baby in prams. Nanda Kaul tries to imagine Ila Das at that stage. Of course she knows Ila Das had been born to a family that could afford prams and ayahs in those heydays of the Empire. Through Nanda Kaul's reminiscence we come to know of Ila Das's history, or the story of her fragmented life. She was unfortunate to have been born with a most unpleasant voice, which had haunted her as a curse through her school life, her early girlhood days, and the later unhappy years of struggle and deprivation. Nanda Kaul had been her only friend to stand by her through thick and thin. And her delight in meeting Nanda Kaul is obvious, though its expression—so shrill and painfully loud—is almost unbearable even to Nanda.

Chapter 3

Ila Das goes on speaking torrentially—a speech and punctuated by shrill cries and terrifying exclamations—complimenting Nanda Kaul on her house, her graciousness, her great grandchildren, even her apricots. Ila Das is funny, comical, ridiculous and even unbearable to the casual onlooker, and Raka is just baffled at her countless exclamations and strange funny ways. She does not know how to respond.

But the reader should not miss one very pertinent observation of Ila Das: 'My dear, you and I are simply bound to be friends, you know, *bound* to be.' The ironical significance of the innocent endearing claim will be brought home to the reader at the end when their inseparable bond, their real affinity beneath all obvious contrasts, will be underlined by Ila's death at the foot of the hill, which will be synchronized with Nanda's death and Raka's fire on the top.

Chapter 4

Nanda Kaul's tea table, Ila Das exclaims, reminds her of all the nice times of the past. When Nanda Kaul tries to protest slightly—as she knows very well nothing in Carignano could remind one of the elegance of that life—Ila Das claims that it is not the material items but the very presence of Nanda Kaul that brings those days back to her mind. She now begins her reminiscence about Nanda

Kaul's parental home, and Raka feels uneasy that the game of impossible stories is going to start anew. But Ila Das does not notice the child's restiveness. She rambles on fantasizing a past in which she assumes they were happy. She even starts a song which is disconcertingly painful to the ears of any listener. Nanda Kaul stops her with the tea.

Chapter 5

Ila Das's song is stopped, but the talks cannot be stopped. She continues to spin her own yarns about Nanda Kaul's marital house. It is a 'waterfall of speech.' Raka wonders in agony if there was no end to 'this tiresome teatime game of old ladies,' this reconstruction of the past. Nanda Kaul, however, does not join the game this time. She seems to have left it to the enthusiastic Ila Das, who would even try to draw Raka into this game. But Nanda suddenly feels it is shameful. She falls silent. The unstoppable Ila Das goes on with her memory-games—the sprawling house, the wonderful garden, the magnanimous host, the brilliant hostess, the delightful summer evenings, the badminton court, the splendid games played threat, the unbeatable partnership between the Vice-Chancellor and Miss David [...]. At this point all the elaborately built up fabric suddenly crumbles. An embarrassed silence follows. Raka looks up in surprise and sees two old ladies, silent, beaten in life, sitting in an abandoned court from which other players have receded.

Chapter 6

Nanda Kaul rises to the occasion and takes charge of the situation in her habitual dignified way. She asks Raka to call Ram Lal for clearing the table, and changes the subject of conversation to Ila Das's village work. Raka at once takes the chance to escape. Now the two old friends can meet each other in harsh honesty, unembarrassed by any memory-making, though both were real and necessary in their own ways. Nanda Kaul knows every turn of the road Ila Das had to take, and how far those turns were from the 'flowery tinkling' years of childhood. By the time Ila Das came to join the university of Nanda Kaul's husband as a lecturer in Home Science, already her father had died of a stroke, her mother had become an invalid, the brothers who had been sent to foreign universities had squandered all the family savings without getting a degree. Ila Das and her sister, the two hardworking daughters were left to fend for themselves and their invalid mother as best as they could. Nanda Kaul had seen those two sisters, two 'horrifically ugly, hideously handicapped girls' showing the worth of their upbringing. Rima started giving piano lessons from house to house in addition to looking after the ailing mother. For Ila Das she had secured this job for a brief period, and that was the only blessed period of Ila Das's fife, about which she speaks so nostalgically. Ila Das had to leave the place after the death of Nanda Kaul's husband. Since then it has been from worse to worse until Nanda Kaul sent her information about a course in social service which eventually led to this small job on the Himalayan foothills among very poor rustics. At last Ila Das has once again come back to Nanda Kaul's place, but only to realize that Nanda Kaul had lost her hold on things, she had mentally retired, had withdrawn.

Chapter 7

Nanda Kaul tries to reach out to her distressed friend from the distance of her retirement. She asks if Ila is managing to make both ends meet. This is honest heart-to-heart talk. Ila Das candidly admits how hard it has been in the recent years, with less and less people going for piano lessons, and Rima getting increasingly more helpless with her cataract, and Ila has to support both her sister and herself with her meager income. She realizes it is their upbringing—supposed to be one of the best in its time—that has made them specially helpless.

In this brief chapter talk becomes punctuated with silence, which is weighed down with the sadness of shared memories of frustration and betrayal, failure and bitterness.

Chapter 8

Ila Das, with her indomitable spirit, quickly recovers herself, and even tries to laugh at the thought of her comparative well-being when seen side by side with the life of the poorest, who are also victims of horrid superstitions and evil customs. In this context Ila Das tells Nanda Kaul about her attempt to stop child marriage and how this has angered some people with vested interest in the locality. She speaks of one Preet Singh who has turned hostile to her because of her effort to prevent the marriage of his child-daughter to an aged widower with six children.

Nanda Kaul feels worried at this disclosure and asks her to be careful. This, again, is ominous and proleptic. In spite of the best of care that she can take Ila Das will not be able to get back home. She will be raped and murdered for her sincere and serious efforts to forestall an inhuman child marriage—the marriage of Preet Singh's child-daughter to a rich old landowner.

Chapter 9

Nanda Kaul and Ila Das, standing side by side, as Nanda sees Ila off at the gate, make an odd contrastive pair. Nanda Kaul is erect, elegant, dignified in her silk, while Ila Das is small, shriveled, funny, jerky in her very little movement and speech.

While they come down the steps and Ram Lal is busy with the tea things Raka sneaks in for a moment unnoticed by anybody, snatches the match box from the table and disappears.

The brief chapter serves as a link to important forthcoming events. This is going to be the last meeting and last separating of the two old friends. They are not only standing at the gate of Carignano, but metaphorically speaking, they are also standing just on the threshold of another gate, *i.e.* the gate leading out from the house of life into the dark endless valley of death. Of course they do not know of their imminent death, and in this last picture framed by evening twilight and pine trees of the Carignano gate, the two old ladies emerge as a pathetically charming pair, so vulnerable yet so blissfully and ironically unaware of the catastrophe waiting by the next turn of the road.

Chapter 10

At last Ila Das leaves and Nanda Kaul is left alone to her solitary house. After the noisy evening she feels relieved; but at the same time Nanda Kaul has apprehensions about Ila Das who seems so defenseless, so vulnerable. Nanda Kaul thinks she has never seen anyone 'more doomed, more menaced' than Ila. She watches over the dwindling figure of Ila down the road. But during this hour at least there is no one, neither a boy nor a langur, to disturb her on the deserted road. She feels relieved once again. Now she begins to walk in the garden waiting for Raka.

This is the brief deceptive pause and lull preceding a devastating catastrophe. Anita Desai finely evokes this brief peace which will be shattered soon and the contrast will make the finale all the more effective. This is an instance of her aesthetic sense of artistic economy and symmetry.

Chapter 11

Chapters 11 and 12 take us further down the hillside as Ila Das trudges back toward her hut down the hills. Even on this deserted road a boy riding a cycle shouts some angry insult, a passing jeep leaves her covered with dust, while some school-girls jeer at her discomfiture. Ila Das pretends to ignore these assaults; but does she not feel the sting? But nobody seemed to understand her excepting the grain seller, an elderly whiskered man, very clean and decent; he seems to feel a little for her, to understand her feelings, her sensitivity and innate self-respect. He tells her not to be so late, not to walk alone in the dark. Although Ila Das pretends defiance, she is afraid nevertheless. Watching Ila Das plodding her way homeward in the growing dark, the kind grainseller feels uneasy. The grainseller's feeling is as much an indication of his sincere solicitations for Ila Das as it is a comment on the social insecurity of women, even old women like Ila Das.

Chapter 12

Ila Das hurries homeward. She is tired. She is hungry. She knows there may not be much or anything to eat in the dingy room she lives in. She still thinks of it as her home. Reaching home she will light her small lamp. This single thought inspires her to go along, when a black shape springs from behind the last rock between her and the village. Preet Singh rapes and strangulates Ila Das. She lies there—crushed, raped, broken and killed—in the dark.

The incident shows how ferocious a man can be when one's mean, selfish interest is affected. Ila Das turns out to be absolutely helpless against the corrupt and reactionary forces of the society, against brutal male chauvinism.

Again, although Ila Das is not young or beautiful or attractive in anyway, although she is just a withered old woman who has been beaten and tattered by life, Preet Singh must rape her before murdering. This is a reflection on the masochistic nature of male violence which, when targeting a woman, must add insult to injury. Murdering Ila Das, therefore, is not enough. She must be stripped first, cruelly and vulgarly violated, and only after that be strangulated to death.

Chapter 13

In this last chapter of the novel Anita Desai is at one of her best feats of artistic excellence.

The telephone rings at Carignano. Nanda Kaul feels reluctant to answer. Then Ram Lal comes out of the kitchen, and calls her; it is her phone. It is from the police station carrying the news of Ila Das. The police asks her to come to the police station and 'identify.' While holding the receiver Nanda Kaul takes a plunge within, and identifies herself with Ila Das. Ila Das had been stripped before being killed. Nanda Kaul strips herself of all the delusions, all the dream houses, all the myths she had so carefully adorned her stories with. She stands face to face with naked truth, and dies holding the receiver.

In the meantime Raka has come back to tell Nani that she has set the forest on fire. This is the first time that Raka insistently calls her Nani, but she gets no response.

Outside the flames spread through the forest.

Thus the novel ends on a symbolic note.

4

Themes

The Woman's Predicament

Anita Desai has said about her work: "My novels are no reflection of Indian society, politics or character. They are my private attempt to seize upon the raw material of life." However, women constitute the bulk of this material. It is the predicament of women, usually in the Indian context, that continues to be the focus of Desai's novels.

In 2001 Anita Desai said,

> Specially in my earlier work I found myself addressing the same things over and over again: very much about the life of women who are confined to home and family, also the solitude from which a person can suffer even if living within a big family or surrounded by crowds.

These very words can be used to sum up Nanda Kaul's experience in *Fire on the Mountain.*

Anita Desai is known for her sensitive portrayal of the inner life of her female characters, especially as they are trapped in the interminable meshes of daily life as the caretaker and nourisher and the what-not of the family. Several of Anita Desai's novels explore tensions between the family members as a collective body, and the sensitive woman as an alien individual.

Eventually she would develop a more inclusive canvas. On being asked in an interview of 2001 about the subjects she should prefer writing about, the author said:

> Specially in my earlier work I found myself addressing the same things over and over again: very much about the life of women who are confined to home and family, also the solitude from which a person can suffer even if living

> within a big family or surrounded by crowds. But after several years and several books I began to feel suffocated myself by the confinement of these subjects. I felt I was limiting the territory to such an extent that it created a kind of suffocation even for me. So I very deliberately opened my doors, to widen the canvas, and started writing more about male characters and their lives, because I felt they had a wider experience of the world, and I could address a greater variety of experiences.

In some of her later novels Anita Desai has also dealt with such themes as German anti-Semitism, the demolition of traditions, and Western stereotypical views of India as the 'Other.'

Basically, however, Anita Desai is concerned with a profounder subject and a challenging target; it is a 'search' for the hidden 'meanings' underneath the apparent 'meaninglessness' of so-called 'real' life around us. She seems to be carrying the legacy of Virginia Woolf on her shoulder when she observes:

> One's preoccupation can only be a perpetual search for meaning, for value. For—dare I say it—truth. I think of the world as an iceberg—the one-tenth visible above the surface of the water is what we call reality, but the nine-tenths that are submerged make up the truth, and that is what one is trying to explore. Writing is an effort to discover and then to underline, and finally to convey the true significance of things.
>
> (Interview with Yashodhara Dalmia)

Anita Desai's reply to the questionnaire of the *Kakatyia Journal of English Studies (1978)* further clarifies her stand regarding the issue.

> My writing is an effort to discover, underline and convey the significance of things. I must seize upon that incomplete and seemingly meaningless mass of reality around me and try and discover its significance by plunging below the surface and plumbing the depths, then illuminating those depths till they become more lucid, brilliant and explicable reflection of the visible world.

In *Fire on the Mountain* we have this wide canvas on which we can identify some of her recurrent themes. For example, it is the claustrophobic life of the woman in an Indian family that still occupies her attention in addition to the helplessness of the girl child and the pathetic fate of a poor lonely woman with no adequate means of sustenance and no one to protect.

In *Fire on the Mountain* Ila Das's gruesome death underscores two realities. One of these is the helplessness of the girl child, which is still a continuing reality in the far flung and orthodox spheres of our society, where she is often just a commodity to be transacted between two males.

Ila Das's murder, again, underscores the mean violence of vengeful male chauvinism when it feels threatened, even by an innocent well-meaning woman, even when she is frail, old and harmless like Ila Das. It furthermore reveals the extent of this masochism which is satisfied with nothing short of the meanest and cruelest humiliation that can be perpetrated on a woman. So Preet Singhs in this world are not content with the murder of an innocent fragile unprotected old woman; they must rape her before killing.

Apparently Ila Das has nothing in common with Nanda Kaul; neither in their respective appearances or temperaments, nor in the kind of life each has lived, or the way people behave with them. Still they can be seen as replicating each other where both of them are victims. Behind the tall, elegant stature of Nanda Kaul, there crouches, as it were, someone as humiliated and "defeated," as helpless, insignificant, vulnerable, small and pitiable as Ila Das. It is the shock of this perception that finally kills Nanda Kaul when she is summoned by the police station to come and "identify" the mutilated body of the dead woman.

Again, Ila Das and Tara, in their different ways, illustrate the predicament of women to whom life can be too hard and unkind.

Woman and 'Space'

In *Fire on the Mountain* Anita Desai captures a woman's dream of a 'space' of her own. All along her life the protagonist had been denied a space of her own; but in the last years of her life she is allowed the expanse of a mountain.

The hill station resort of Kasauli, to which Nanda Kaul retires in her old age is a real empirical space, and at the same time it is emblematic of Nanda Kaul's silent protest and assertion. At last she gets 'a room of one's own' *(a la* Virginia Woolf) on this mountain. It is a contrast to the male spaces she had lived in in the past, spaces which were occupied and controlled by her father and husband respectively. Coming here "on the ridge of the mountain" she feels she has reached "the place [...] she had wanted and prepared for all her life" (3). It gives her "a great, cool flowering of relief" (3) and she wants "no one and nothing else" (3).

The difference between Nanda Kaul and Raka is the difference between two generations of women on either sides of a century regarding the outlook on a 'space' of theirs. However, it is their common attachment to the mountain that makes them true blood relations, and makes the child a true inheritor of the old woman's 'space.' Nanda Kaul has been ravaged and then rejected by life; Raka is "a bird fallen from a nest fallen from a tree." Nanda Kaul longs to be a pine on the hill; Raka burrows into it like an insect. And together they enable us to grasp the meanings and the suggestions of the mountain as a space, a sign, a trope in the context of the novel.

The traditional male/colonial way of seeing a place has been to see it as a 'virgin' woman. Contrastively, Nanda Kaul and Raka do not try to possess or appropriate or reconstruct/re-inscribe the place. They just want to get merged into the place like a tree or an insect. The author's treatment of mountain as space thus becomes an emblem of her *ecriture feminine* and thus offers the possibility of fresh, varied, contrary and multiple interpretations.

During the early phase of postcolonial writing in India the authors often used carefully built constructs which could serve as microcosms for the Indian 'space.' That was also a way of asserting the nationalistic ego. 'Malgudi' or 'Kanthapura' is a typical example of such construct, which stood for the lovable and loved Indian space as envisioned and projected by the authors. It was a proud, almost emphatic way of inscribing one's own space. A similar assertion was also to be found in the poetry of expatriate Indian poets in the post-independence decades, including Ramanujan, Parthasarathy, Ezekiel, *et al.*

The discourse of 'space'—so prominently figuring in postcolonial writing—attains a new dimension in the hands of two successive generations of women writers in India. These writers reflect a search for a space of 'her' own, as an individual in 'her' own right. This, of course, falls in pattern with the slow but steady emergence of women in various walks of life since independence. Again, this is also in tune with the global trend in women's writings across the world about 'Her Story.'

However, in India the journey has been an uphill one; because the society is still largely governed by patriarchal ideologies and norms. It is interesting to note how the women writers in India, especially since the last three decades of the last century, have been giving voice not only to their own aspirations, ordeals, anguish and frustrations, but also to those of the previous generations—of their mothers and grandmothers. One of the many ways of expressing this consciousness is giving voice to the longing for a space of 'her' own, or the anguish at failing to find one. Thus, whereas the importance of 'Kanthapura' or 'Malgudi' was apparent to the affective and experiential modalities of a traditional culture, Indian women writers, since the, seventies, have inscribed the Indian landscape with new meanings, signs and signals. As Mary Conde puts it in her essay, "Women Inscribing the Indian Landscape":

> Lacking the titillating consciousness of writing fiction-driven fiction about an imperial possession, Indian women writers inscribe Indian landscape with moral criticism, sadness, entrapment—or simply dreariness. (141)

Kasauli in *Fire on the Mountain* thus emerges to be a 'sign,' signifying the desire of women to be and become individuals without constriction or limitation.

The desire to escape into some ideal utopian space of freedom takes Sita, the protagonist of Desai's novel, *Where Shall We Go This Summer?*, to her childhood island. Ironically, for Uma (*Fasting, Feasting*), there is neither a mountain nor an island to escape from the prison of her parental family. Still she has an occasional dream of escape, though nowhere to escape to in real life.

> Her vision of an escape, a refuge, took the form of a huge and ancient banyan tree with streaming gray air roots, leafy branches in which monkeys and parrots bleated on berries. Sometimes she heard the berries raining down on the zinc roof [...]. Then she saw herself seated on a stone step, listening to the parakeets in the banyan tree, looking out at that flash of water in the sand and the kites hovering in the sky so high above that they merged with infinity. (1999: 131)

Children

Although a mother of many children, a time comes in Nanda Kaul's life when she cannot think of a child around her; she feels a child should be an anachronism in Carignano. Carignano is like her; it is complete, and has stopped to evolve. A child means evolving, growing up, change, effort at renewal, at addition. She simply does not want to become anything any more. Hence she cannot reconcile herself to the vision of a child around Carignano.

> She could no more picture a child—in this perfected and natural setting than she could a pergola of roses, a marble faun or a fountain. She wished for none of these. On the contrary, the thought of them sickened as a box of sweets might sicken. (31)

Nanda Kaul has been a mother of many children. But when she remembers the past in its aspect of endless childbearing and childrearing, the memory does not seem to give her any pleasure. Rather she remembers this as an exhausting duty at best.

> She thought of her sons and daughters, of her confinements, some in great Discomfort at home and others at the small filthy missionary-ryn hospital in the bazaar, and the different nurses and doctors who had wanted to help her but never could, and the slovenly neurotic ayahs she had had to have because there was such a deal of washing and ironing to do [...].
>
> She seemed to hear poignant shrieks from the canna beds in the garden—a child had tumbled off the swing, another had been stung by a wasp, a third slapped by the fourth—and gone out on the veranda to see them come wailing up the steps with cut lips, bruised knees, broken teeth and tears, and bent over them with that still, ironic bow to duty that no one had noticed or defined. (18-19)

On the eve of death Nanda Kaul admits to herself "her children—the children were all alien to her nature. She neither understood nor loved them" (145).

When Raka is just thrust upon her Nanda Kaul is seriously annoyed; but eventually she would realize Raka's difference from all the children she had ever known, and she mentally accepts Raka even to the extent of considering her as the most natural and appropriate inheritor of Carignano. Indeed, Raka is an unusual child by any standard. She is not sweet, not charming, nor playful, dependent, or demanding in any way. Still she comes to manifest the author's vision of childhood as a pure, uninhibited, uncorrupted condition. It is because of her independent, genuine spirit of truth and detachment that she can win over Nanda Kaul.

In Desai's *Clear Light of Day* a character comments on the acute sensitivity of a child.

> 'No one,' said Bim, slowly and precisely, 'comprehends better than children do. No one feels the atmosphere more keenly—or catches the nuances, all the insinuations in the air—or notes those details that escape elders because their senses have atrophied, or calcified.'

It is through the child's eye that the truth or falsity of a thing becomes exposed. The child as the seer, or the perfect mirror, has been a paradigm with a long literary tradition to back it up. Even in cultural traditions we had glimpses of a divine child figure, like baby Jesus, or *balagopal* Krishna. But usually this wise progeny has been envisioned as a male figure. Anita Desai, in her projection of Raka, thus strikes a departure from a long tradition by upholding a girl child as the seer and pioneer figure in her novel.

Arundhati Roy too, in her celebrated novel *The God of Small Things* (1997), uses two innocent children's (a girl and a boy) perspective to bring home to the reader the sadness and cruelty of a hypocritical adult society.

Critical Responses

Basavaraj Naikar has rightly remarked:

> Of all the contemporary Indian English novelists Anita Desai is, perhaps, the most perceptive and consistent explorer of the inner life, especially that of Indian women, convulsed by an acute sense of helplessness in the face of the onslaughts of an unfeeling world and the resultant mental agony. (Naikar 72)

According to N.R. Gopal also one of the distinguishing features of Anita Desai is that

> she tries to introduce a modern psychological vein and projects a sensibility generally not encountered in other Indo-Anglian writers of fiction. As a novelist her distinguishing qualities are many, the chief among them being the subordination of the background to the

> characters and the deft handling of language, imagery and syntax in order to convey an intimate expression of the inner world of her characters. She insists on analysing her characters and the story is important only in so far as it reflects the obsessions of her characters. Free from the journalistic enthusiasm for depicting the socio-political life in India, Mrs Desai makes each work of hers a haunting exploration of the psychic self. The work is executed so thoroughly that her treatment gets the look of a philosophical system—a system which has been familiar to the world in the form of "Existentialism" [...]. (Gopal 5)

Gopal places his special critical emphasis on the psychological dimension of the novel. As he stresses:

> In Desai's stories action is subordinated to psychology. The central themes revolve around the mental and spiritual developments of the dramatis personae and not on their physical adventures. This relegation of action to a secondary place enables us to understand more profoundly the how and why of a situation. In this respect the writer shows a close affinity with Virginia Woolf who also entered the consciousness of the characters and showed little concern for the actual outside action. The theme of Desai's novels like that of the novels of James Joyce and Virginia Woolf, is human nature and human relationships. Her stories are peopled with men and women such as we see around us and with happenings such as might occur any day to such people. The central theme of man-woman relationship with which Desai deals has been treated by several other Indian writers like Nayantara Sehgal, Nargis Dalai, and Kamala Das. But in Desai the themes are governed by existential tones. The existential perspective on the theme of individual and society is evident in all the stories. By way of definition, it may be said that the main themes dealt with by the existential thinkers are those of alienation, despair, frustration, anxiety and the emotional life of the individuals. In the words of F.H. Heinemann, "The problem of existentialism is in a narrower sense expressive of the present crisis of man, and in a broader sense, of the enduring human condition." (Gopal 10)

It is also worth recalling what Dr S.P. Swain has to say about the theme of existentialism in Anita Desai's novel. Swain writes in his article "Note of Existentialism in the Novels of Anita Desai":

> A modern philosophical movement, Existentialism deals with man's disillusionment and despair. Originating in the philosophical and literary writings of Jean-Paul Sartre, it was more an attitude to life, a vision, or what Kaufmann calls a "timeless sensibility that can be discerned here and there in the past" (Kaufmann 12). A philosophical idealism, existentialism, in due course of time developed into a powerful revolt against reason, rationality, positivism and the traditional ways in which early philosophers portrayed man. Man's autonomy, assertion of his subjective self, his flouting of reason and rationality, positivism and the traditional ways in which early philosophers portrayed man. Man's autonomy, assertion of his subjective self, his flouting of reason and rationality, his denial of traditional values, institutions and philosophy, his exercise of 'will' and 'freedom,' and his experience of the absurdity and the 'nothing-ness' of life are some of the existential themes which are reflected in the writings of the exponents of existentialism.
>
> Anita Desai's chief concern is human relationship. Her central theme is the existential predicament of the individuals projected through the problems of the self in an emotionally disturbed milieu. Delicately conscious of the reality around them, her protagonists carry with them a sense of loneliness, alienation and pessimism. Desai adds a new dimension to the genre of Indian fiction in English by probing the unquestionable existentialist concerns of her protagonists. Toeing the line of the existential humanists, to Desai, existentialism means "the mad or bad [...] the shocking, the sordid or the obscene" (Grene 01). Anita Desai is obsessively occupied with the individual's quest for meaning and value, freedom and truth that provide spiritual nourishment to the estranged self in a seemingly chaotic and meaningless world.
>
> The search for identity on the part of the existential self in Desai assumes a socio-psychic dimension. The Desai protagonists do not shy away from the assaults

of existence. Existential heroes, they face the problems of life single-handedly with courage and determination. Experiencing disgusting absurdity of the world, they discover meaning in self-immolation or self-affirmation in "a world irremediably absurd where one is a stranger to oneself as well as to other people" (Cruickshank 52).

Desai's novels from *Cry, the Peacock* to *Journey to Ithaca* are a study in the depth and persistence of human affliction, inexorably sensitive and loving and compassionate as her protagonists are. Existential conflicts in Desai spring from the self's craving for the fulfilment of certain psycho-emotional needs, from the desire to overcome the horror of separateness, of powerlessness and of listlessness.

Cry, the Peacock depicts existentialism in its deep-seated morbidity through the neurotic and hysterical self of Maya pining for companionship [...].

All the three major characters in *Voices in the City* are tortured by their hollow existence. Nirode is a rootless character drifting directionlessly, shifting from one goal to another, finally faced with a void, a sense of emptiness. He experiments with failure like a true existential hero. Wearied by his own unsureness, "he swept back and forth like a long weed undulating under water, a weed that could live only in aqueous gloom, would never rise and spring into clear day light." His existential search for meaning and value in life ends in emptiness and bankruptcy.

Like Nirode, Monisha too looks for loneliness and longs for privacy. She prefers non-existence to a meaningless existence. She fails to relate to the reality of her life. The Amla seeks to opt out of the absurd into a life of parties, dinners and dances. Yet hollowness dogs her. Nirode, Monisha and Amla are not concerned with simple problems of work-a-day existence since the journeys they make are essentially spiritual.

In *Bye-Bye, Blackbird,* we notice Desai's existentialist concern rooted in expatriate experience. Ostensibly concerned with the lives of Indian immigrants in England, the novel explores the existentialist problems of alienation, adjustment, rootedness and the final decision in the lives of the three major characters—Dev, Adit and Sarah. It is scattered in numerous symbols and images revealing Desai's irresistible existentialist musings [...].

Where Shall We Go This Summer? is Desai's "shortest existentialist novel" (Prasad: 60). As in *Cry, the Peacock,* here too, Desai very remarkably voices "the terror of facing single-handed the ferocious assaults of existence" (Dalmia, *The Times of India:* 13), through her recurrent, favourite existential theme of husband-wife alienation [...].

Fire on the Mountain limns out the existentialist problems and predicaments of the middle class people, particularly women. Tired of a life of duties and responsibilities for so long, Nanda seeks refuge in the sequestered life of an undisturbed privacy, that of "a charred tree trunk in the forest, a broken pillar of marble in the desert, a lizard on a stonewall." Nanda's problem is the predicament of one exposed to a protracted life of unrelenting routine. She is left with little nerve for anything save a wish to have a sigh of relief in peace. The image of the prey and predator (a hoopoe pouncing upon a grasshopper and stabbing it to death) projects itself to the human world through the rape and murder of Ila Das. Here, Desai repeats the animalistic existence of the contemporary society despite the progress of civilization, a theme which occurred in *Where Shall We Go This Summer?* [...].

In *Village by the Sea* existentialism occurs rather thinly. Here, through the life of a young village boy Hari, Desai captures the existential predicament of the ruralizes undergoing the pangs of a society in transition. [...]. (101-105)

Swain further argues:

Critics like Solanki and R.S. Sharma have often observed that the Desai protagonist is a psychologically fragmented individual who relies chiefly on indirect methods of coping with a stress situation which ventilates through various survival strategies. Escape, withdrawal and a denial of reality seem to be prominent primitive survival strategies among the Desai protagonists. But is the self only psychologically fragmented? I would rather attribute

> the laceration of the self in the Desai protagonists to their emotional shocks which manifest in various modes of psychological observations. Hence, the individual in Desai novels is both emotionally and psychologically disturbed. But can human existence be solely identified in terms of intellect only? It would be better to call the Desai characters emotionally malformed and socially isolated. Unreason, in Desai, manifests in the world of absurdity. Ujwala Patil attributes Ila Das's rape and murder in *Fire on the Mountain* to Preet Singh's desire to humiliate her for the injury she had caused to his male ego; but it is rather a manifestation of an individual's cannibalistic and canine existence. It is an assertion of male chauvinism on the part of Preet Singh. In many of the Desai novels the language and imagery have a subjective existential tone. Most of the protagonists adopt the existentialist, heroic posture necessary to face the ordeals of life. Anita Desai adopts the decadent type of existentialism that borders on nihilism. The existentialism in Desai's novels is not philosophically disturbing as in the novels of Raja Rao. It is intellectually engaging and poetically captivating as in the novels of Shashi Deshpande [...]." (107)

Thus Swain makes us realize that the novel is meant to be an elaborate verbal evocation of the special kind of existential anguish experienced by old women irrespective of the facade of a high social status. The fact that Nanda Kaul was a Vice-Chancellor's wife just does not make any difference. Existential anguish makes a person feel alienated—alienated from the society, alienated from the family, and finally alienated from one's own self as it would be gradually evident when Nanda Kaul would begin to have recourse to myth-making. But that myth will be finally exploded and she will land into utterness and die of the unbearable shock.

5

Characters

In her "Replies to the Questionnaire" (*Kakatiya Journal of English Studies,* 3: 1, 1978) Anita Desai said that she was concerned not with "the one-tenth visible section of the iceberg that one sees above the surface of the ocean but the remaining nine-tenths of it that lie below the surface." The author further admitted that her endeavour was to discover the significance of reality by "plunging below the surface and plumbing the depths, then illuminating those depths till they became a more lucid and brilliant explication of the visible world."

According to Jasbir Jain, Anita Desai "probes deep into the inner recesses of the psyche of the character and delves deeper and deeper in a character [...] rather than going around it" ("Desai Interviewed," *Rajasthan University Studies in English*).

In an interview with Yashodhara Dalmia in 1979 Anita Desai said:

> I am interested in characters who are not average but have retreated, or been driven into some extremity of despair and so turned against, or made a stand against, the general current; it makes no demand, it costs no effort. But those who cannot follow it, whose heart cries out 'the great No', who fight the current and struggle against it, know what the demands are and what it costs to meet them. (*The Times of India,* 29 April 1979)

While discussing Desai's *Clear Light* [...] Dieter Riemenschneider observes:

> Thus by directing her explorative beam of light deeper and deeper into their lives, the past of her adult characters, Desai reveals more and more of their true selves to us and

> to themselves. *(The New Indian Novel in English,* Ed. Viney Kirpal. 1990: 198)

This applies in particular to Nanda Kaul and Ila Das in *Fire on the Mountain.*

Nanda Kaul

Fire on the Mountain is the story of women. At the centre there is Nanda Kaul, an elegant lonely old woman. Nanda Kaul is by no means the type, common, run-of-the-mill Indian woman. She is unique in her elegant isolation. She is thin and straight like the pines of Kasauli, high and empty like Carignano, where she retires alone after her long and busy career as wife and mother.

Nanda Kaul maintains a stance of proud indifference. Nanda's house is up on a steep hill. Whereas people much younger than her toil up the steep path, "bent-backed," with difficulty, Nanda Kaul "always made a point of keeping her back as straight as a rod when walking up that path" (11). This indicates her nature, her proud stoicism.

However, behind this facade she hides a deep frustration. It is a sense of utter futility, and an overpowering desolation that haunts her even at this old age.

Nanda Kaul had developed the habit of caring, a patriarchal value which is automatically internalized by Indian women. They are born to, and brought up within the stronghold and stranglehold of this patriarchal culture. But eventually she would realize the futility of all this caring and nurturing.

> The care of others was a habit Nanda Kaul had mislaid. It had been a religious calling she had believed in till she found it fake. It had been a vocation that one day went dull and drought-struck as though its life-spring had dried up.
>
> It had happened on her first day alone at Carignano. After her husband's death, her sons and daughters had come to help her empty the Vice-Chancellor's house, pack and crate their belongings and distribute them, then escort her to Kasauli. For a while, they stood about, in Carignano, like too much furniture. She had wondered what to do with them.

When they leave it is a relief to her.

> Fortunately, they had gone away. Brought up by her to be busy and responsible, they all had families and employments to tend. None could stay with her. (31)

Nanda Kaul is not interested in the garden, its sparse fruit, the nestlings in the nests. It is significant that she does not enjoy watching the scene of the mother-bird feeding the chics. "It was a sight that did not fill her with delight. Their screams were shrill and could madden. She prefers instead "the knoll, the topmost height of her garden, where the wind was keenest and the view widest."

Carignano, the house and the garden, has been likened to Nanda Kaul, as if it is an extended metaphor for the old lady.

> Like her, the garden seemed to have arrived, simply by a process of age, of withering away and an elimination, at a state of elegant perfection. It was made up of a very few elements, but they were exact and germane as the strokes in a Japanese scroll. She no more wished to add to them than she wished to add to her own pared, reduced and radiantly single life. (31)

As the novel opens, Nanda Kaul has already arrived at Kasauli, and her hill station house 'Carignano'; and she seems to have found a sort of contentment. It has, as it were, reached a fulfilment of a life-long dream:

> Everything she wanted was here, at Carignano, in Kasauli. Here, on the ridge of the mountain, in this quiet house. It was the place, and the time of life, that she had wanted and prepared for all her life—as she realized on her first day at Carignano, with a great, cool flowering of relief—and at last she had it. She wanted no one and nothing else. Whatever else came, or happened here, would be an unwelcome intrusion and distraction. (3)

Nanda Kaul at Carignano is the recluse who has apparently done away with the demands of life, and now she wants to be left alone. She does not even want to receive letters or messages. Even the sight of the postman fills her with annoyance and she only hopes that the postman will not stop at Carignano; because the postman suggests a connection with the world below the mountain, along with its various demands, calls, impositions, botherations, which she thinks she has left behind for ever. The novel opens on this note of renunciation and withdrawal:

> Nanda Kaul paused under the pine trees to take in their scented sibilance and listen to the cicadas fiddling invisibly under the mesh of pine needles when she saw the postman slowly winding his way along the Upper Mall. She had not gone out to watch for him, did not want him to stop at Carignano, had no wish for letters. The sight of him, inexorably closing in with his swollen bag, rolled a fat ball of irritation into the cool cave of her day, blocking it stupidly: bags and letters, messages and demands, requests, promises and queries, she had wanted to be done with them all, at Carignano. She asked to be left to the pines and cicadas alone. She hoped he would not stop. (3)

At the beginning we are told that all Nanda Kaul wants at this fag end of her life is "the sound of the cicadas and the pines" (19). The other sound acceptable to her is the music of the withered rose-creeper in Carignano, which is "an exhausted mass of grey creaks and groans" (17). Does she find an extension of herself in it?

It is, however, significant that although Nanda Kaul prefers the hilltop view from her veranda, finds it "more comfortable," she would also often go round to the back of the house, and gaze "down the gorge with its gashes of red earth, its rocks and gullies and sharply spiked agaves, to the Punjab plains— a silver haze in the summer heat—stretching out to a dim yellow horizon" (17).

At such moments she is also reminded of "all those years she had survived and borne" (17). And she sees those years in the metaphor of the gorge: "like the gorge, cluttered, choked and blackened with the heads of children and grandchildren, servants and guests, all restlessly surging, clamouring about her" (17). Here is a subtle suggestion that in spite of her apparent withdrawal from the plains and from her past life there, she still carries these other spaces within her consciousness; later in the story she would weave her fiction— "memory-making" (123), around these spaces.

The following passage from Simone de Beauvoir's observations on the plight of 'the married woman' seems to be particularly relevant in studying Nanda Kaul's personality, and in understanding her deliberate posture of a stiff withdrawal.

> A [married] woman determined, in spite of her condition, to go on living in a clear-sighted and genuine manner may have no other resort than a stoic pride. Being in every material way dependent, she can know only an inner, abstract freedom; she refuses to accept readymade principles and values, she uses her judgment, she questions, and thus she escapes conjugal slavery; but for her aloofness, her fidelity to the rule: 'Bear and abstain,' constitute but a negative attitude. Imobilized, in renunciation and cynicis, she lacks positive employment for her power; she aids others, protects, gives, does this and that; but she suffers from finding no truly demanding task, no real aim. Consumed in her solitude and sterility, she may deny and destroy herself. (Beauvoir 495)

Again, Nanda Kaul at Carignano, seems to fit amazingly to Beauvoir's description of the predicament of the old woman in her concluding paragraph to the chapter "From Maturity to Old Age" *(The Second Sex):*

> Old women take pride in their independence; they begin at last to view the world through their own eyes; they note that they have been duped and deceived all their lives; sane and mistrustful, they often develop a pungent cynicism. In particular, the woman who 'has lived' knows men as no man does, for she has seen in man not the image on public view but the contingent individual, the creature of circumstance, that each man in the absence of his peers shows himself to be. She knows women also, for they show themselves without reserve only to other women: she has been behind the scenes. But if her experience enables her to unmask deceits and lies, it is not sufficient to show her the truth. Amused or bitter, the wisdom of the old woman still remains wholly negative: it is in the nature of opposition, indictment, denial; it is sterile. In her thinking as in her acts, the highest form of liberty available to the woman parasite is stoical defiance or sceptical irony. At no time of her life does she succeed in being at once effective and independent. (607-08)

Ila Das

Ila Das represents another aspect of a woman's ordeal in a sexist society. Her father spends all the money on the sons' education, who turn out to be worthless and irresponsible. Ila Das gets an education which comes to no use when earning becomes a dire necessity. Still she shoulders the responsibility of her mother and sister.

Ila Das is pathetically unconscious of her own unattractiveness,—her ugly appearance, repulsive voice, and ridiculous gestures. Nevertheless, she suffers from the knowledge that she is a laughingstock for everybody, big and small. Even Nanda Kaul, who has known her so long, finds her company unbearable. The street urchins jeer at her, and are more cruel in teasing this hapless, ugly, deformed old woman than the street dogs or the *langurs* of Kasauli. Finally she is raped and murdered just because she had tried to prevent a child marriage. Yet she is just an innocent well-meaning frail and simple woman.

Ila Das represents a fragmented life. She is an individual, and at the same time she represents a type, the origin of which can be traced back in the colonial past of the country. She was born and brought up in apparent affluence. But eventually all this affluence and the Anglicized upbringing proved to be sadly illusory and useless. And Ila Das ended up in a life of hard struggle for bare survival. That too was finally terminated by rape and murder of the helpless woman.

As Nanda Kaul tries to envision the baby Ila, "the shrivelled old lady in miniature, propped up against lace-edged pillows in a sky-blue pram [...],"

> About the pram and lace she was certain. Nanda Kaul's family had known Ila Das's in the days when some of the glory of the British Empire was allowed to reflect on a few favoured natives. Such families lived in large bungalows on quiet roads. In their houses sherry was served before lunch, port after. Their servants wore white cotton gloves. The ladies went for evening drives along the river, at first in creaking carriages, later in pompously purring automobiles. So of course there had been a sky-blue perambulator, too, and an ayah to push it importantly under the jacaranda trees, and a skirted nanny to time its

> promenade on a great china-saucer watch presented to her by her employers. (110)

The author points out:

> This was the contradiction in Ila Das's life that irked Nanda Kaul—it was the piece of gravel that insisted on slipping into her shoe and out of it. Ila Das's life was simply not all of a piece—Nanda Kaul had seen so many pieces of it, littered over the northern plains, and here was the last broken bit, spiked by an agave beside the path leading to Carignano. (110)

Thus, Ila Das comes to represent a broken fragmented life and identity, which Nanda Kaul alone perceives. Others— from children to adults—continue to jeer at her, heckle her, and harass the poor creature in various ways.

It is only Nanda Kaul who can remember Ila Das as the small girl, the child of an affluent and upper-class family, brought up in the typical Westernized fashion of those days as were supposed to be appropriate for a girl child in such a family. She remembers her "lisping the nanny-goat-and-pinafore rhymes that western and westernized babies speak" (111). While staring at the bald white scalp of the old friend struggling uphill in the afternoon heat—she tries to imagine "Ila Das as an infant in an afternoon frock of blue ribbons and white lace, screeching the most unimaginably horrid sound that sent shivers down the spines of guests and relatives invited to hear her recite her nursery rhymes" (111). Nanda Kaul remembers how "she and Ila Das had played together as children," "had gone to school together, solemnly cycling down the quiet roads to the convent" (111). Ila had her own piano, a gift from her parents, and had piano-lessons accordingly, though she had, of course, no musical talents, and a very unpleasant voice which made her a common laughing stock.

By the time Ila Das comes to visit Nanda Kaul at Carignano Nanda perceives in her the "last little broken bit of a crazy life, fluttering up over the gravel like a bit of crumpled paper" (112).

Both Ila Das and Nanda Kaul are victims. Apparently there is no similarity between the two women; apparently they are contrasts to each other in respect of appearances or temperaments, in the kind of life each has lived, or the way people behave with them. Still they can be seen as bound to each other by some deeper tie; it is to be seen where both of them emerge as victims. Behind the tall, elegant stature of Nanda Kaul, there crouches, as it were, someone as humiliated and "defeated," as helpless, insignificant, vulnerable, small and pitiable as Ila Das. It is the shock of this perception that finally kills Nanda when she is summoned by the police station to come and "identify" the mutilated body of the dead woman. With the brutal death of Ila Das, the violent world outside which she had carefully pushed back from her consciousness at Carignano, bounces back once again and shatters her shell. Now she can "identify" herself with Ila Das.

Again, there is another vital kinship between Nanda Kaul and Ila Das; both are myth-makers. Both Nanda Kaul and Ila Das try to construct a make-belief world of "memory-making." They do this not only to please Raka, but also as it were, to seek a refuge for themselves, to seek some sort of solace or comfort from myth-making, when real life provided little scope for dreams or happy recollections.

Raka

Critics have usually seen Raka either in relation to Nanda Kaul with whom she has both interesting affinities and significant differences, or as a metaphor of ruined childhood and a victim of circumstances in which her mother continually suffers from the cruelty of her husband and leads a very unhappy conjugal life.

However, Raka emerges to be the most unique person in the novel. Of course, one might say, 'Oh, she is just a child!' But even as a child, Raka is not a very common childlike child.

Raka, the great granddaughter of Nanda Kaul, is the child of a broken home. The child has been appropriately described as "a bird fallen out of its nest, a nest fallen out of a tree" (50). For a child of her age, Raka is remarkably withdrawn and self-sufficient. Immediately after coming to Carignano Raka gets friendly to the place. Quietly she settles down into the house and the place as if she were just another insect or small bird of Kasauli.

Raka, to say the least, is not a normal or average child. As a child she is necessarily dependent. But "Raka herself remained totally unaware of her dependence, was indeed as independent and solitary as ever."

> Solitude never disturbed her. She was the only child Nanda Kaul had ever known who preferred to stand apart and go off and disappear to being loved, cared for

> and made the centre of attention. The children Nanda Kaul had known had wanted only to be such centres: Raka alone did not. (79-80)

For Raka the house is more than a brick and mortar thing. In a profound way she comes to belong to the house, to get intimate with it. Raka likes the house as the best of all the places she has been to. It has been a smooth and easy entry for Raka.

> She had not been asked to Carignano. Yet here she was, fitted in quietly and unobtrusively as an uninvited mouse or cricket. (80)

Raka appears to be the right 'inheritor' or descendant of Nanda Kaul. And once Nanda even feels she would leave the child the legal inheritor to the house, since she was the only one among all her kins who would have understood the spirit of the house. Raka has been what Nanda would have been.

But then Nanda also understands that "Raka no more needed, or wanted, a house than a jackal did, or a cicada" (103).

The strange child seems to be remarkably courageous in her peaceful loneliness as well as her stubborn refusal to find solace in the lure of false myths.

Again, Raka also feels strangely drawn by the burnt house on the hilltop. Raka feels a queer fascination for the fire, and the relics of past fires. She would every now and then come to the burnt house on the hill, and would imagine as if she were turned into a pine tree in flames.

> She raised herself onto the tips of her toes—tall, tall as a pine—stretched out her arms till she felt [...] she was alight, ablaze. (91)

The child climbs over the ruins and stands still in the "scorched, empty" room (90); she listens to the murmuring silence and the demented birds that

> [...] beckoned Raka on to a land where there was no sound, only silence, no light, only shade, and skeletons kept in beds of ash on which the footprints of jackals flowered in grey. (90)

Raka is not attracted by the nurseries and bedrooms of her infancy, nor by the clubs and parks of the big cities. She likes Carignano much better than all these other places; she admits to herself, "it was the best of places she'd lived in ever" (91).

Still the neat and orderly place seems to her a bit confining. In contrast, "it was the ravaged, destroyed and barren spaces in Kasauli that drew her" (91). Accordingly, a burnt cottage or the eerie silence of an abandoned house appeals to her more.

> This hill, with its one destroyed house and one unbuilt one, on the ridge under the fire-singed pines, appealed to Raka with the strength of a strong sea-current—pulling, dragging. There was something about it—illegitimate, uncompromising and lawless—that made her tingle. The scene of devastation and failure somehow drew her, inspired her. (90)

Is it because she is the child of a broken home that Raka is so drawn to the sites of broken or burnt or abandoned houses?

Raka also possesses the innate clarity of an unspoilt child, and thus she can see through the pathetic memory-making of the old women. In this connection we are reminded of what another character of Desai says:

> 'No one,' said Bim, slowly and precisely, 'comprehends better than children do. No one feels the atmosphere more keenly—or catches the nuances, all the insinuations in the air—or notes those details that escape elders because their senses have atrophied, or calcified.'

This passage from *Clear Light of Day,* (1980) another novel by Desai, seems to be particularly applicable to Raka. Raka can see through the fantasy or memory-making of Nanda Kaul, and she is bored by it, while she longs for her lonely freedom on the mountains. As Nanda Kaul goes on inventing stories in praise of the fantasized figures of her own father and husband:

> Raka sighed and twisted aside to see if Ram Lal would not come and release her from this disagreeable intimacy [...]. She would have to break out into freedom again. She could not bear to be confined to the old lady's fantasy world when the reality outside appealed so strongly.
>
> She thought desperately, with longing, of the charred house on the ridge, of the fire-blasted hilltop where nothing sounded, mercifully, but the creaking of the pines in the wind and the demented cuckoos, wildly calling.
>
> And here she was hedged, smothered, stifled inside the old lady's words, dreams and more words. She yawned with boredom. (100)

Raka's final act of setting the mountain on fire appears to acquire rich symbolic overtones in the context of the story.

Raka and Nanda

Nanda Kaul clearly perceives the similarity as well as difference between Raka and herself *vis-à-vis* the mountain. They are similar in the sense that both want "only one thing—to be left alone and pursue her own secret life amongst the rocks and pines of Kasauli" (48).

At the same time, Nanda Kaul is also conscious of the difference in their respective responses to this space to which both have come for shelter.

> If Nanda Kaul was a recluse out of vengeance for a long life of duty and obligation, her great-granddaughter was a recluse by nature, by instinct. She had not arrived at this condition by a long route of rejection and sacrifice— she was born to it, simply. (48)

Nanda understands the difference and she appreciates and admires the child for being what she herself could not be. The relationship between Nanda and Raka, the elegant old lady and the semi-orphaned emaciated child, the great-grandmother and the great-granddaughter, can be considered from a wider perspective.

As one goes through Margaret Atwood's poems one feels how this 'other' within the self becomes increasingly a conglomerate image which becomes a contraction and coinciding point of generations of women. One may cite the following lines from Atwood's "Five Poems for Grandmothers":

> Sons branch out, but
> one woman leads to another.
> Finally I know you
> through your daughters,
> my mother, her sisters,
> and through myself. *(Selected Poems II* 14)

This is assertion—or better to say, wishful thinking—of a common heritage,—of a matrilineal line of ancestry and belonging. Indeed, for centuries, and millenniums, we have spoken of 'ancestors,' but not of 'ancestresses.' It is this foremother or ancestress, in place of 'forefather' or 'ancestor,' who has been emerging as a new icon in *ecriture feminine* across the globe today, Canada and India being no exception.

Way back in 1932 Dorothy Livesay (b. 1909) makes a loving, nostalgic invocation to the 'grandmother' in her poem "Green Rain." As memory surges back, the image of the grandmother becomes the overwhelming sign of all that had been dear and treasured:

> I remember long veils of green rain
> Feathered like the shawl of my grandmother [...]
> I remember the road [...]
> [...] which leads to my grandmother's house,
> A warm house [...]
> And the silence, full of the rain's falling
> Was like my grandmother's parlour
> Alive with herself and her voice, rising and falling—
> Rain and wind intermingled. [...]
> Now I remember the day
> As I remember my grandmother.
> I remember the rain as the feathery fringe of her shawl.
> [*The New Oxford Book of Canadian Verse.* 134]

It may also be interesting to recall in this context the following lines from Sylvia Plath's "All the Dead Dears" (*The Colossus*):

> From the mercury backed glass
> Mother, grandmother, great grandmother
> Reach me, hug hands to have me in.

The relationship between Nanda and Raka—great grandmother and great granddaughter—can be considered in the light of this emerging paradigm in women's writing across the globe, connecting generations of women along a matrilinear matrix.

Tara and Asha

On the other hand, Asha and Tara, mother and daughter, taken together, present a contrasting paradigm in which the connection proves negative and unsupportive, because Asha has internalized patriarchal values, and therefore fails to be supportive to her daughter in her crises.

Asha, Tara's mother and Nanda Kaul's daughter, manages to be happy by means of shallow blitheness, a careless bluntness to things and issues. But Asha's daughter Tara breaks down under the oppressive pressure of an unbearable marriage.

Asha has been introduced in the novel through Nanda's point of view, as the mother remembers her daughter. Still it is not a very pleasant impression anyway. Whereas Tara suffers from a loveless marriage and would cling only to her sick daughter,—Asha complains, "all she does is sit by Raka's bed and read her stories" (15). Asha does not seem to understand her daughter's feelings or suffering. Even Raka knows better. She has "known her mother ill for most of her life, mysteriously ill, mostly in bed, under a loose pink blanket that smelled of damp, like the lilies" (89). In her nightmares she would wake up imagining her mother crying under the torture of an abusive husband. "Somewhere behind them, behind it all, was her father, home from a party, stumbling and crushing through the curtains of night, his mouth opening to let out a flood of rotten stench, beating at her mother with hammers and fists of abuse—harsh, filthy abuse" (71). But Asha would rather side with Tara's husband.

> The least loved or, at any rate, the most exasperating of her [Nanda's] daughters. Asha, the beauty, had dedicated her life to the cultivation of long, glossy hair and an unwrinkled skin and had had little time left over for her unfortunate daughter, the one who married a diplomat and, as a result of his ill-treatment of her, the affairs he had, his drinking and brutality, was reduced to a helpless jelly, put away out of sight and treated as an embarrassment who could, if she tried, pull herself together. (14)

Asha cannot simply understand "why shouldn't she [Tara] be happy." She is sure "The main thing [...] was for Tara to rouse herself and make another try at being a successful diplomat's wife" and since Tara's husband would be getting a new posting at Geneva, "Geneva would be an excellent place for such an effort" (14). Therefore she, in her blunt self-assurance, would persuade Tara to pack for Geneva and pack off Raka to Carignano.

In this context one is reminded of Maya's disillusioned thinking about marriage in Anita Desai's novel, *Cry, the Peacock*. In her unhappiness Maya can see issues in better clarity, and thus realizes:

> It was discouraging to reflect on how much in our marriage was based upon a nobility forced upon us from outside, and therefore neither true nor lasting. It was broken repeatedly, and repeatedly the pieces were picked up and put together again, as of a sacred icon with which, out of the pettiest superstition, we could not bear to part. (1963: 40)

But Asha is not Maya; she has not attained clarity through pain and suffering. It is perhaps not unexpected that Asha's insensitive efforts should prove futile, and Geneva should prove no better than any other place for Tara, who has been broken repeatedly in the past, and now broken once again. As Nanda has to reply to Raka's query about her Mama:

> She's ill again [...] she's in a nursing home again, in Geneva. (88)

Tara typically fits into the crushed woman paradigm. Yet her suffering does not seem unreal. She is never the assertive subject, but is rather the passive object in the sentence of family life. And she has been appropriately portrayed through other's memories or opinions, which only serve to highlight her passive status. Raka often remembers her mother with a feeling of miserable, helpless sadness, while Asha is impatient with Tara for the very reason for which Nanda Kaul remembers Tara with empathy. The reason is Tara's inability to blunt the edge of her sensitiveness, and thus put up with life however gross and brutal it may be. Nanda Kaul herself had to put up with much in her own life; and behind the facade of her dignified posture as the vice-chancellor's wife there was also a trampled self like Tara hiding all the time, which has been finely suggested by the image of a crumpled shuttlecock in the deserted badminton court in the vice-chancellor's house. Is it because of this that Nanda Kaul feels so sympathetic towards Tara; at one point she even thinks of leaving Carignano to Tara who, Nanda feels, might need the shelter some day.

Again, Nanda Kaul's one single memory of Tara is that of a happy child enjoying the sudden burst of flowers on the hill after a night of rain. This is subtly suggestive as it throws up the glaring contrast between a delightful and excitable girl, and the despondent, crushed, broken woman,—the state to which the happy girl can be eventually reduced.

Other By-standers

Minor figures like Ram Lal, "the Carignano cook," the postman, the truant school-boy, the pony man, the sympathetic grain seller, *et al.,* come alive through vivid little touches. We get just one glimpse of the grain seller as Ila meets him on her last walk down the hills; but he leaves a fine impression of a man who is simple and humble, but essentially good and decent. The grainseller is the only man in the valley to understand and feel for Ila's suffering. The man, who is not even given a name, comes up vivid through just one or two brush strokes.

> The grainseller—an elderly, whiskered man in a singlet and very clean, white cotton pyjamas—sat idly sifting pulses through his fingers [...]. He looked benevolently at Ila Das bending over the open sacks. He knew Ila Das.
>
> Whenever she got her salary, she came to his shop for what were supposed to be her month's provisions, only the shopkeeper knew they couldn't possibly last more than a fortnight—not even for such a child-sized and time-shrivelled creature. He would always throw in a free handful of red chillies or some cloves of garlic which was generous of him for they were expensive. She [...] made him feel kindly towards her. His own daughter was club-footed—why should he laugh at this poor creature's deformities? (137)

He feels worried and concerned for the poor woman.

> He said suddenly, 'Are you going home now, Memsahib?'
>
> 'Yes,' she said, surprised, stopping to look at him. 'You shouldn't go so late,' he said, and his face was troubled behind the profusion of whiskers. 'It is not good for a memsahib to walk alone in the dark.' [...] He did not say anything more, only shook his head and kept an eye on her as she made her way back through the bazaar with her empty bag [...]. (138)

He feels uneasy at remembering Preet Singh's remarks on Ila Das.

> He thought of Preet Singh who lived in the same village as Ila Das and had passed the time of morning earlier today and spoken of Ila Das, how she was trying to stop him marrying off his daughter to a rich landowner who had made a good offer. Preet Singh had spat and

> cursed Ila Das, using coarse, obscene words that made the grainseller fall silent in disapproval. He himself knew a Memsahib when he saw one. Such obscenity upset him as a badly cooked meal might. Watching Ila Das clumsily pick her way through a marble game in the road, he frowned with uneasiness. It was growing dark. (138)

Thus the grainseller offers a contrast to the coarse, chauvinist criminal Preet Singh. One feels a sort of mild reassurance, that at least everybody is not Preet Singh although ultimately it is the Preet Singhs who have their way in this society. People like the grainseller or Ram Lal are there, representing the common humble people who are not schemers or villains, but are ineffective though sympathetic kind-hearted men.

Critical Responses

Expectedly critical opinions have generally veered round the three principal characters: Nanda Kaul, Ila Das and Raka, the two old ladies and the child.

About Anita Desai's art of characterization R.K. Gupta writes in "Art of Characterization," the 5th Chapter of his book on the novels of Anita Desai:

> Mrs. Desai makes each work of hers a haunting discovery of the inner psychic self. It may be said that in the 50s and 60s Existentialist philosophy had become quite fashionable among flowering urban intellectuals. Mrs. Desai selects its theories to her structure. Desai's characters are neither common and ordinary nor their problems are related with food, clothes and house, as the novelist herself writes:
>
> I am interested in characters who are not average but have retreated or been driven into some extremity of despair and so turned against, or made a stand against, the general current. It is easy to flow with the current, it makes no demands, it costs no effort. But those who cannot follow it, whose heart cries out "the great No" who fight the current and struggle against it, they know what the demands are and what it costs to meet them.
>
> Desai's female characters are generally neurotic, highly sensitive but alienated in a world of dream and fantasy, separated from their surroundings as an outcome of their

> failure or unwillingness to adjust with the reality. They always differ in their ideas from others and venture on a long voyage of contemplation in order to trace out the meaning of their existence. An author pointing out the psychological aspects of characters has to employ a certain design by which the interior working of the protagonist's mind is unfolded to the readers gradually with the progress of the narration [...]. (Gupta 183-84)

Gupta studies the characters in *Fire on the Mountain* from the above perspective. He holds:

> In the novel *Fire on the Mountain* the principal characters as well as the situations have been designed to dramatise and demonstrate these fundamental truths of human existence. A close perusal of Anita Desai's novel explains that her characters have peculiar childhood. In an interview [with Jasbir Jain] the novelist herself says that "I agree that the experiences of childhood are the most vivid and lasting ones." Mrs. Desai has confidence that childhood experiences are lasting and play a vital role in the development of a wholesome personality of the characters.
>
> This is the only novel of Mrs. Desai in which nature plays a vital role on the level of symbolism, imagery and metaphor and it has to be assumed that she makes effective use of this technique to depict different characters. The title has its symbolic meaning. It also points out the nature symbolism. The 'fire' and the 'Mountain' both are natural occurrence. The fire is known as an instance of man-made, to be more specific Raka made it. The Mountain is itself natural.
>
> The protagonist of the novel, Nanda Kaul, has central attraction, lives in a house called Carignano at Kasauli after the death of her husband. Nanda Kaul, widow of Vice-Chancellor who is compelled both by choice and circumstances to live in alienation in an old house on hill-station. The novel makes the use of fantasy and it is Nanda Kaul who lives in the world of fantasy. She is leading a lonely life, and is attended by an old servant named Ram Lal. She wishes to be alone throughout her very busy life as a wife and as a mother of several children. She desires

to pass her rest time of her life peacefully in a solitary confinement. She gets very angry even at the sight of the postman coming to her house, and tries to conceal herself from him in the garden wishing:

[...] She could merge with the pine trees and be mistaken for one. To be a tree, no more and no less, was all she was prepared to undertake.

These lines indicate the inner feeling of Nanda Kaul to become a tree is symbolic. It symbolises that she wants to live a free and solitary life having no attachments to anyone. She finds the "barrenness" and emptiness of Carignano which is the emblem of the vacuum and emotional barrenness of her life. Shyam Asnani, a reputed critic argues that, "Anita Desai is perhaps the only Indo-English novelist who lays stress on the landscape and correlates it with the psychic state of her protagonists." Mrs Desai's heroines are all obsessed with their inner states and their trouble affects their all responsibilities and reflections. Here Nanda Kaul sees herself as the yellow rose creeper which is creaking and moaning. The use of metaphors is highly suggestive for a proper illustration of the total sensational make-up of the characters. The other ornamental use like alliteration and onomatopoeia are also used.

The house of Nanda Kaul with its past history and background is highly suggestive. The house is "simple and white and shining on the bleached ridge." The white colour is the emblem of death and despair. The house was built by Colonel Macdougall to protect his wife and seven children from heat but all died in the house. The stained nature of the house is also portrayed through different householders who reside in the house one after another. Nanda Raul's life is symbolically depicted through a creeper hanging on the wooden railing:

[...] the yellow rose creeper had blossomed *so* youthfully last month but was now reduced to an exhausted mass of grey creaks and groans again.

The creeper shows Nanda Raul's life—she led a life which was full of incidents and she bore several children, but at present she is old, grey and lonely. The creeper symbolises the temporal nature of young age in the novel.

Nanda Raul maintained her marital life very well, she performed all the duties of a housewife but neither husband nor her children understand her perturbed life. This indifference compelled her to pine for a privacy. Her inner desire is symbolically presented through an eagle:

> An eagle swept over it, far below her, a thousand feet below, its wings outspread, gliding on currents of air without once moving its great muscular wings which remained it repose, in control.

The eagle is the emblem of complete separation here: a free soul that is not bound by any responses or duties, and is not concerned to any place or person. Shanta Rrishnaswami as a critic points out, "the debunking of the myth of motherhood runs as a continuous thread in Anita Desai's novels." No other woman novelist portrays the character of a mother in such sickly and offensive images as Mrs. Desai does.

Nanda Raul feels very old all of a sudden. Raka's arrival compels her to think that she is quite aged. Raka finds her grandmother very much like the pine trees in the garden. They embrace each other, but because "they felt they must." Raka is stranger to the hill and she walks in her room "as the newly caged, the newly tamed wild ones do." But Raka goes out to move and see the outside scenery to discern its beauty, angle and interest. It indicates that Raka moves and sees the realities of life which lie beneath the external beauty. The dust-storm moving from the plains to the mountains is also symbolic. It shows materialism. The selfishness and materialism of the people from town are growing stronger to perturb the hills also. It also indicates that the dishonest and mean qualities of man highly impress the innocent, good and gentle people.

Raka's alienation suggests that she is above obedience, discipline or the duties of life. But she also experiences that she is "shipwrecked and alone." This indicates her familiar discord and disharmony. Her parents are not living in harmony and hence she is with her grandmother. The strayed family background compels her to think that she is "alone in my boat on the sea, she sang." She desires to live alone, concealing herself from the people of her surroundings. This very plight of Raka disturbs Nanda Kaul though she herself lives in alienation and she is not doing it out of choice, there is no other way left for her. But for Raka it appears as if she were a born worshipper of loneliness. Nanda Kaul tries to remind the figure of Raka and her environment. Her memories flashed before her mind's eye and she remembers the days when she has tended her own children and grandchildren—Asha, Tara, Vina and their offspring too. The outlook of Raka's arrival at Carignano fills Nanda Kaul with a little dread and annoyance. "How could she sleep with someone else in the house."

The extraordinary characteristic quality of Raka appears almost a kindred spirit to Nanda Kaul. Raka suits into the environment of Carignano as an 'uninvited mouse' or a 'cricket.' Raka's concern with the spirit of the place makes Nanda Kaul think:

> Would she own it herself one day, Carignano? Nanda Kaul wondered, lashing her fingers together over her chest. Ought she to leave it to Raka? Certainly it belonged to no one else, had no meaning for anyone else. Raka alone understood Carignano, knew what Carignano stood for—she alone valued that, Nanda Kaul knew.

The novel depicts the characteristic state of Ila Das, who captivates as well as repels Nanda Kaul's tender sensibility. Ila Das, a committed social worker by profession, shows quite contrast to Nanda Kaul. Ila Das and Nanda Kaul have been friends from childhood and their families too were closely related. Nanda Kaul's past is full of sadness whereas Ila Das's present is marked by shameful and painful events. Ila Das suffers and leads a poor, insecure life, she represents lofty values of lift like nobility and humanity. Though she is not able to look after herself properly, she shows unending concern and love for the poor. She has been facing with penurious problems, becomes a welfare officer and is posted in the hills. Ila Das prohibits and opposes the orthodox wedding of Preet Singh's seven years old daughter to a farmer who is a widower with seven children. This is the reason by which Ila Das is brutally raped and murdered by Preet Singh in an act of inhuman retaliation. Her life symbolises the tragic life of a woman in our society. This plight of women in our society suggestively paints through the different character. Ila Das, Nanda Kaul and Tara—all suffer in one way or another at the hands of men. The birth of revolt against man and the cruel world is symbolically described by Anita Desai in these words:

With a sudden spring, she rose and went flying down the knoll, the bright sparks at the ends of her dry hair flying like flames in the wind [...].

Nanda Kaul's granddaughter Tara also suffers from a maladjusted marriage. A pattern of Tara's neurosis comes out clearly through Asha's letter. It is a common picture of unhappiness: Colonel Macdougall, a companion and nurse-maid to his sickly wife and children, waiting for death, leaking out to the cemetery and the horrified Pastor and his mad, killer of a wife, whose total life is a race between the prey and predator. Nanda Kaul's conjugal life is also a bitter instance and this critical situation forces her to accept seclusion. Her marriage is purely based on corporal lust and situational convenience for the man. Mr Kaul also keeps his beloved Miss Davidson, a teaching staff. Nanda Kaul becomes a mother of several unwanted, unloved children. In spite of this, to her, everything appears to be smooth outwardly but inwardly she burns with the fire of suffocation and frustration. The familiar situation is not adjustable and hence Raka is also obsessed by the circumstances and tried to live in seclusion. She roams and wanders in the forest freely and peacefully knowing the impending danger in it. The novel ends at the death of Ila Das, Nanda Kaul and setting fire in the forest by Raka. Raka's past image here establishes. The 'evil' atmosphere at home has bruised the 'child,' Raka. All the images of cage, violence, isolation and morbidity with reference to Raka are justified. This image offers insights into Raka's abnormal psyche.

In Anita Desai's fictional world it is always through some inanimate or non-human representatives that inner acts of the characters are made clear, never by direct statement. Every occurrence in the external world is depicted a graphic illustration and a symbolic significance of the characters. This way, it is an indication of the rebel of the neo-class of woman against the man-dominated world

> and Raka herself appears as a symbol of this neo-class of feminine sensibility [...]. (Gupta 203-07)

B. Brahmananda Chary looks upon Raka as a metaphor for ruined childhood. Chary writes:

> Raka of *Fire on the Mountain* is perhaps the most complicated and mysterious child character in the entire gamut of Indian fiction in English. She presents an intriguing picture to the readers by her unusual behaviour. Raka means the moon. But Raka, the character, is not round faced, calm or radiant. In fact, animal imagery is profusely used to describe her in the novel. To her greatgrandmother Nanda Kaul, she appears like "one of those dark crickets that leap up in fright but do not sing, or a mosquito, minute and fine, on thin, precarious legs." Raka's "extravagandy large and somewhat bulging eyes" (39) make Nanda Kaul feel more than ever her resemblance to an insect. Besides, she has "large and protruding ears (40) [...]". (Chary 88)

The critic makes a perceptive analysis of Raka's nature;

> Raka has the gift of avoiding what she regards as dispensable. Gradually, Nanda finds Raka to be "the finished, perfected model of what Nanda Kaul herself was merely a brave, flawed experiment" (47). Like her, Raka does not love company: "She had not a dog's slavishness to companionship" (56). She outrightly rejects "the very thought of school, of hostels, of discipline, order and obedience" (59). She has a non-conformist and detached self.

With her undemanding nature and independent existence, Raka leaves Nanda wondering what an extraordinary child she is. No normal child will be like Raka. She "was not like any other child she (Nanda) had known, not like any of her own children or grandchildren. Amongst them, she appeared a freak by virtue of never making a demand. She appeared to have no needs" (47). She seems to have given up all the childhood pleasures and desires. Children of her age often have stock interests: fairy tales, adventure stories, flowers, butterflies and the like. Raka, on the contrary, regales in ugliness, danger and destruction. Her imagination is weird and she is irresistibly drawn to strange things.

If a child finds the world hostile, the easiest course for her is to withdraw from it. But, Raka instinctively learns to expect nothing from it. There is no move on her part to participate in life, to strive for achievement and to socialize. That is perhaps why the rocks, symbolising lifelessness, attract her. She has lost what Rollo May calls "internationality" (In Bande, 223) meaning the faculty of entertaining intentions with the help of which one can relate oneself to the world.

To Raka's unusual behaviour is added to craving for setting something on fire. When Ram Lal expresses his fears about the human being knocked over and the fire being spread, Raka asks him in excitement: "Will it set fire to the garden? [...] Will it set the hill on fire?" (53). She has a mysterious urge to see fire on the mountain. Her desire for destruction is symbolic of the burning rage within herself. It is a secret yearning for a companion who is akin to her, not with an interest to share or bear the wilderness of her life but as a consolation. The deprivation of loving care has created disturbance in her subconscious mind making her emotionally blank and inclined to set the world on fire. Raka is a victim of 'Emotional deprivation," to use a phrase of Leland H. Scott. Usha Pathania also rightly says that Raka's "embarrassing, loveless childhood fills her heart with distrust and suspicion. She, therefore, turns her back upon human beings and their so-called safe, cosy and civilized world and develops a strong fascination for the ugly, lonely, rugged and desolate aspects of nature" (In Dhavan III 210) [...].

Any normal child would want the company of an elder while visiting tourist spots or other places. But Raka never likes such company. She wants to do everything on her own. For example, while going to Monkey Point, Raka does not want her great-grandmother to accompany her.

> She had planned to come to Monkey Point alone, on a solitary afternoon expedition, without anyone's knowing, secrecy was to have been the essence of it, she relished it so—Raka had all the jealous, guarded instincts of an explorer, a discoverer, she hated her great-grandmother intently watching her ascent, clenching her hands with tension when the goats nearly knocked her off her feet or when she slipped on the loose pebbles (60-61). (Chary 89-90)

By any standard Raka is no common child, and the critic highlights this aspect of Raka's personality:

> [...] it becomes evident that Raka has a strange fascination for being left alone. She even takes delight in being not cared for at all. When she is at the top of Monkey Point she feels "light and exhilarated, airborne as a seed or a blade of grass" (61). Quite extraordinarily, Raka takes delight in imagining that she does not have anyone and she is all alone: "I'm shipwrecked, Raka exulted, I'm shipwrecked and alone. She clung to a rock—my boat, alone in my boat on the sea, she sang" (61-62). This quality in Raka disturbs Nanda Kaul and makes her think: "Raka's genius. Raka's daemon." (64)

The way Raka moves about in the dark makes her appear queer and strange. It is impossible for any normal child—for that matter even adult—to wander about in the dark like Raka does. She finds darkness, rather than light, friendlier to her. She is at home with the things of the darkness and is afraid of the "hairy young men" of the club because there is something "some alarming about them, to her, than in the wails of jackals or the sudden rattles of the night jars in the darkness" (68). It is abnormal that laughter and happiness do not appeal to Raka. They instead appear to be repulsive to her. On being encouraged by Ram Lal, Raka goes to the club to have the vision of "ladies dressed as queens and men as princes" (68). But when she peeps into the ballroom, she is shocked. She thinks that the scene is lunacy rampant. The drumming of the band and blowing of paper horns frightens her:

> She wished she could close her eyes. She wished she were a million miles away from the band. She tried to think she was asleep and this was a nightmare (69). Raka flees this scene like an animal being pursued, sobbing the while, "*Hate* them—*hate* them [...]." (71).

The perverted acts of the people dressed in a bizarre fashion unlock the hidden memories of her own father and his wild behaviour at home:

> Somewhere behind them, behind it all, was her father, home from a party, stumbling and crashing through the curtains of night, his mouth opening to let out a flood of rotten stench, beating at her mother with hammers and

> fists of abuse—harsh, filthy abuse that made Raka cower under the bedclothes and wet the mattress in fright [...] and her mother lay down on the floor and shut her eyes and wept. Under her feet, in the dark, Raka felt that flat, wet jelly of her mother's being squelching and quivering, so that she didn't know where to put her feet and wept as she tried to get free of it. Ahead of her, no longer on the ground but at some distance now, her mother was crying. (71-72)

Raka comes back to the world of reality only when a jackal howls. After the club incident, a peculiar change comes over her thin, pale face:

> Her eyes darkened, as if with a secret she would not divulge. She was no longer the insect, the grasshopper child. She grew as still as a twig (72).

However, Raka does not stop going to the ravine to wander. She moves about chanting defiantly under her breath:

> I don't care—I don't care—I don't care for *anything!"* (73)

Raka is drawn to the fire, when she sees it for the first time: "Shivers ran through her, zigzag, leaving streams of sweat in their wake" (74). During that night she keeps "getting out of bed and coming barefoot into the drawing-room to look out of the window and see the fire spread" (75).

One may think that Raka is cold towards Nanda Kaul and does not want to develop intimacy with her because of her (Nanda's) reserved nature. But the textual evidence shows that Raka does not have intimacy even with her mother. She does not miss her in the least. She does not feel home-sick. She moves about in Carignano as if as lived there ever since her birth.

This strange attachment on Raka's part to the place may be interpreted as her way of forgetting all the suffering associated with her home and parents. "Her traumatic childhood" says Shanta Krishna Swamy, "has hardened her into a hard little core of solitary self-sufficiency and now recovering from a bout of typhoid, her spirit is defiant enough to go chanting" (Swamy 273). Intimidated since birth, anything destructive, lawless, uncompromising and ruthless excites her. Krishna Swamy continues: "The conventional sweet smells and sounds of childhood are ignored, she feels drawn by scenes of devastation and failure. The forest fires tingle her and she bursts from the shell of Carignano like a sharp keen-edged explosive to set fire to the mountains" (Swamy 262).

Childhood is a formative period when a person has intrinsic desires for spiritual health. The child discovers the beauty and sweetness of human relationships through love. Raka's parents have no time or inclination to fulfil her emotional needs. Her mother Tara is in such an unhappy predicament that she cannot do anything to help Raka. Her shattered mental equilibrium and deteriorating physical strength render her helpless. Her father has not time to look after her well-being. Consequently, Raka's "Traumatic experiences deprive her of child's innocent trust and feeling of joy in the company of others" (Pathania. In Dhawan III 209). With the result, unlike other normal children, she is not interested in stories about people, about relations. Her curiosity about people and what they do has been blunted [...].

Raka is a victim of an unwholesome, empty and hopeless childhood environment. She spends her childlhood and develops her consciousness in a home which reeks of disease and moral decay. Her mother is sick forever and father is found drinking at all hours. They are just not worried about the emotional growth and adjustments of Raka. Such an unhappy home environment creates fear, insecurity, distrust and anxiety in growing children. For healthy growth, a child needs an orderly and secure world. For creating order, parents-child exchange of ideas is essential. Discussing the positive influence of a harmonious familial interaction upon the psyche of a growing child, Sudhir Kakar comments: "An individual's identity and merits are both enhanced if he or she has the good fortune to belong to a large, harmonious and close knit family" (Kakar 121). For Raka, childhood means a nightmare, violence and terror, because she has seen them taking place in her house and they have left an indelible impression of her tender consciousness. It is because of this, when Nanda Kaul tells about her childhood as being happy and her father being affectionate, Raka concludes that they are perfect lies. Raka's final act of setting fire to the mountain is then not merely an act of violence, but also an act of purification as it might burn away the lies and the make-believe world of Nanda Kaul and the mental agony of her own.

Raka alleviates her suffering by resorting to violence. It is a means of escape for her. By the act of setting fire to the forest, she saves her ideal self from being totally destroyed. Like a rubber ball hit hard against the wall, Raka bounces back on the cruel and false world with a vengeance [...]" (Chary 91-95).

N.R. Gopal makes some perceptive observations on the Nanda Kaul-Raka relationship. In the Chapter, "Familial Relatioships" in his book on Anita Desai Gopal writes:

> Nanda Kaul, the widow of a vice-chancellor, is compelled both by choice and circumstances to live in a secluded old bungalow 'Carignano,' in Kasauli, fiercely guarding her seclusion and privacy. But her insulated life is stirred by the arrival of her great grand-daughter Raka, a girl of seven or eight years, an introvert, sensitive as Nanda herself. She is very much confined to her own self, resenting any intimacy with Nanda. She busies herself with rambling through deserted hills and gorges, she is specially attracted towards a burnt house and is preoccupied with the idea of a forest-fire. A childhood friend of Nanda, Ila Das who has fallen on bad days, is a social worker in a nearby village. She comes to tea with Nanda one afternoon. They have long chat about their early days, their experiences as a social worker, and as the vice-chancellor's wife respectively. She now lives in penury. On her way back it gets dark and near her village Preet Singh, who was dissuaded by her not to marry his minor daughter with an old man, is waiting in ambush. Angered by Ila Das's opposition to the marriage, he strangulates her and later rapes her. Nanda is informed telephonically about the outrage by the police inspector. She is still to digest this shocking news when Raka comes to say that she has set the forest on fire. And this is the end of the novel. Anita Desai excels in the poetic portrayal of the locale with charred trees, desolate landscape, dusty road, rain and the like. The novel is full of animal and nature imagery.

Like Lotte, Nanda too could not legally belong to the family and she is no better than a kept. In this case the blame goes to the cowardice of Prof. Kaul who just gave lip service to marital life. Outwardly the Kauls were an ideal couple to university community but from inside it was all empty, the whole social role and socialising was a mere sham:

> Not had her husband loved and cherished her and kept her like a queen—he had only done enough to keep her quiet while he carried on a lifelong affair with Miss David, the mathematics mistress whom he had not married because she was a Christian but whom he had loved, all his life loved.

Because of her husband's cowardice and selfishness Nanda Kaul had to suffer. She readily discharges her duty towards the family but in doing so loses her individuality and identity. Like Sita of *Where Shall We Go This Summer?* Although to a lesser degree, Nanda Kaul is not very happy in coping with the large family and unending stream of guests.

> And her children—the children were all alien to her nature. She neither understood nor loved them. She did not live here alone by choice—she lived here alone because that was what she was forced to do, reduced to doing. (*FOM*, 145)

She is so busy raising the family and discharging the duties of mother, housewife and hostess that in the evening of her life she is happy in her seclusion even though it is partly voluntary and partly circumstantial. When the news of her grand-daughter Raka's arrival comes she hates being disturbed by the arrival of the uninvited guest. It does not matter that the person coming is her own flesh and blood. In the fifth chapter of the novel when she is looking back at her life we find that through and through she is only pretending, wearing a personae, acting a role which is imposed on her. In the following extract the difference between appearance and reality is made very clear. Our apology for this lengthy quotation lies in the fact that aspect of difference between the surface and inner reality is crucial to Desai's thematic thrust:

> Looking down, over all those years she had survived and borne, she saw them, not bare and shining as the plains below, but like the gorge, cluttered, choked and blackened with the heads of children and grandchildren, servants and guests, all restlessly surging, clamouring about her.
>
> She thought of the veranda of their house in the small university town in Punjab, the vice-chancellor's house over which she had presided with such an air as to strike awe into visitors who came to call and leave them slightly gaping. She had her cane chair there, too, and she had sat

there, not still and emptily, but mending clothes, sewing on strings and buttons and letting out hems, at her feet a small charcoal brazier on which a pot of *kheer* bubbled, snipping threads and instructing the servant girl to stir, stir, don't stop stirring or it'll burn, and then someone had to be called to hold the smallest child from falling into the bubbling pot and carry it away, screaming worse than if it were scalded. Into this din, a tonga had driven up and disgorged a flurry of guests in their visiting saris, all to flap their palm-leaf handfans as they sat in a ring about her—the wives and daughters of the lecturers and professors over whom her husband ruled. She thought of that hubbub and of how she had managed and how everyone had said, pretending to think she couldn't hear but really wanting her to, 'Isn't she splendid? Isn't she like a queen?' Really, vice-chancellor is lucky to have a wife who can run everything as she does, and her eyes had flashed when she heard, like a pair of black blades, wanting to cut them, despising them, crawling grey bugs about her fastidious feet. That was the look no one had dared catch or return.

Looking down at her knuckles, two rows of yellow bones on the railing, she thought of her sons and daughters, of her confinements, some in great discomfort at home and others at the small filthy missionary-run hospital in the *bazaar,* and the different nurses and doctors who had wanted to help her but never could, and the slovenly, neurotic ayahs she had to have because there was such a deal of washing and ironing to do and Mr Kaul had wanted her always in silk, at the head of the long rosewood table in the dining-room, entertaining his guests.

Mentally she stalked through the rooms of that house—his house, never hers—very carefully closing the wire-screen doors behind her to keep out the flies, looking sharply to see if the dark furniture, all rosewood, had been polished and the doors of the gigantic cupboards properly shut. She sniffed to make sure the cook was not smoking *biris* in the kitchen and to verify that all the metalware smelt freshly of Brasso.

> She seemed to hear poignant shrieks from the canna beds in the garden—a child had tumbled off the swing, another had been stung by a wasp, a third slapped by the fourth—and gone out on the veranda to see them come wailing up the steps with cut lips, bruised knees, broken teeth and tears, and bent over them with that still, ironic bow to duty that no one had noticed or defined.
>
> Thus in Nanda Kaul's case familial relationship is not genuine although it may appear to be so [...]. (Gopal 35-38)

In the Chapter "Feminine Psyche" of his book on Anita Desai N.R. Gopal argues:

> If Nanda Kaul defends her privacy fiercely Raka too is absolutely independent, satisfied with her own self and never bothering her Nani. She is so self-absorbed that any effort on Nanda Kaul's part to attract her completely fails, even her fantastic tales. She is the most unchildlike child. Nothing appeals to her. She was "the child who never played games." Instead of listening to the fanciful tales from Nanda Kaul she prefers to go out doors all by herself, roaming in the desolate hills and forest. She is obliquely defiant, and she is mistress of herself. Once coming from her usual ramblings through the hills and forests she speaks to herself, "I don't care—I don't care—I don't care for *anything.*" Her unchildlike quality and introvert nature is the result of her traumatic childhood. Once she stealthily goes down the hill to the club of the Research station on a moon-lit night and while she spies on the drunken orgy in the club her mind is flooded with the unpleasant memory of her childhood days, of her drunken father coming home late at night and beating her mother and she hiding somewhere in the room [...].
>
> It is this traumatic childhood experience that has such a dehumanising effect on Raka's mind that she becomes apathetic to finding any interest in childish games and there is nothing childlike in her character [...]. (Gopal 29-30)

It may be worth-while to point out at this stage that in an extremely interesting article **Carmen Concilio** looks at the female characters of *Fire on the Mountain* from a novel perspective and tries to show how the Iconography of the Crone is inscribed in these characters. She writes:

> While in literature both mother figures and young female characters are widely represented, the figure of the Old Crone entails a far more disturbing iconography which nevertheless allows for a fair amount of different representations [...].

The old Crone is a female who stands close to Mahadevi, who is endowed with all sorts of positive and negative aspects, including creation, preservation and destruction. It is particularly on this potential for rejection, abandonment, death and destruction that this paper will focus on. In ancient religions, this powerful and darker figure is symbolically opposed—though equally valued—to the beautiful, sensual, divine giver of birth, light, love and nurture. To describe this dichotomy there is no better image than that of the goddess Kali, in classical Indian mythology, as an emanation of more reassuring female goddesses, such as Parvati, Sita and Sati. First of all, Kali entails both the terrific beauty of a sensual seducer, and the terrible strength of an executioner of men. Iconographically, she is represented with a dark face and two pairs of hands— as remnants of the archaic female trinity. Maid (Kumari), Mother (Mahamaya Devi), Crone (Kali), or Creator, Preserver, Destroyer [...]. Finally, Kali's iconographic representation also entails that conjunction of the powers of love and death, the drives of Eros and Thanatos, that Freud claims as the main attributes of the Goddess of Beauty as well as of the Goddess of Death [...]. Nanda Kaul, shares with the old Crone a certain pride, strong-mindedness, and authoritarian temperament as well as a potential for violence, of which Kali is an extreme representation. "She was grey (4)," says the extradiegetic narrating voice, thus hinting at her old age. Similarly the Crone, the most powerful of the Goddess's three personae, is described as an old woman. According to the ancient trinitarian scheme, the Crone has taken on the character of the "Grandmother." This equivalence between the Crone and the Grandmother can also be extended to Nanda Kaul, who in the first section of the novel is portrayed as reluctantly waiting for her great-granddaughter who is coming to visit her as an "unwelcome intrusion and distraction" [...]. Nanda Kaul's seclusion in the mountains also establishes a further link with the goddess Parvati and her other intermediate emanation as Durga, for Parvati is called "the daughter of the Himalayas," while nearly all of Durga myths associate her with mountains, usually the Himalayas or the Vindhyas.

> Whereas in modern societies, and to some extent also in the traditional Indian extended family, elderly women tend to be marginalised, Anita Desai centres her novel on the character of an old woman, Nanda Kaul, who deliberately chooses a marginal place to live in. Immediately, the old protagonist identifies herself with the "barrenness and starkness (4)" of the surrounding landscape [...].
>
> [Her] radical refusal of her previous but exhausted role as mother and wife (as Parvati, the loving spouse of Shiva) and her solitary retreat into an inhospitable landscape (as Durga, the vengeful warrior) are elements which exemplify what Kamini Dinesh calls "the negation of the role model," thus describing Nanda Kaul as neither a conventional stereotyped character, nor a role model either for readers or for writers [...].
>
> Undoubtedly, a strong propensity to be quickly angered is Nanda Kaul's most typical feature, a trait she obviously shares with Kali. Her straight posture, "for she made a point of keeping her back as straight as a rod (11)," reveals her uncompromising character, her uprightness being the distinctive mark of her double nature, imbued with a numinous fierceness.
>
> [While] Asha personifies the domineering and interfering mother, ready to rush from one of her daughter's household to the other's, apparently Nanda Kaul is the personification of the wise Crone, who lives in seclusion and in isolation. Yet, here the trinitarian scheme is further developed, for if Nanda Kaul is the old, barren and dry woman, her daughter and granddaughter represent two different kinds of mother-figures, while her great granddaughter, Raka, is the image of the unconscious maiden. Four generations of women are thus represented in this novel, though the narration mainly focuses on Nanda Kaul and Raka, the old Crone and the (only apparently) inexperienced Maiden.
>
> Little Raka is immediately identified as an intrusion and a distraction, because all Nanda Kaul "wanted was to be

alone (17)." Yet, she has to accept the role of "universal educator of the young" which is proper of elderly women. Besides, in her being mother of mothers and fathers, in her intellectual, though silent defence of Tara's rights against her violent husband, and in her acceptance of Raka as if in her lap, Nanda Kaul might also be assimilated to the Goddess Durga of the Hindu Vedic pantheon, as she who is Inaccessible, the Leader of the Mothers, who contains within herself her counterpart: Kali the dark-faced [...].

By the way, the old Crone is often associated with wisdom, her totem being the wise owl, a bird symbolising enlightment. Nanda Kaul preferably identifies herself with the eagle, less in its rapacious attitudes than in its elegance, regal superiority and self-sufficient independence. Furthermore, "in all cultures, flying was the archetypal model of the soul's journey to heaven," such an ability is also attributed to the Crone. Nanda Kaul poses her attention on the hovering flight of the eagle, thus hinting to her own eternal and final flight: "She had wished, it occurred to her, to imitate that eagle-gliding, with eyes closed (19)." However, while the eagle symbolises the eternal dimension of time, and therefore of life after death, the cuckoo seems to be an expression of the real time, specifically Nanda Kaul's present death-in-life. It cannot be a chance that Nanda Kaul reads Gogol's *Dead Souls* [...].

Nanda Kaul speaks with relief about her loneliness, as if it were a conquest, afraid that her great-grandchild's arrival could spoil her tranquillity. For Kasauli is described as a place of light and space, where "hills melted into sky, sky into snows, snows into air (28)," a place that her husband, a scholarly man who read many languages, had liked to call the *"Abendleuchtung* (28)." The German world *Abendleuchtung*, meaning "dusk," hints at the sunset. The hour of "cowdust," also engenders an allusion to the time of the day when the Gods can descend on the earth and mingle with human beings, thus attributing to Kasauli an eerie atmosphere. Kasauli is the place where sky and earth meet, where the soul's final flight is easier for the sky is closer. Similarly, Nanda Kaul's solitary presence in such a landscape and her dreams of flight once again allow for her iconographic stigmatization as Durga.

The second section of the novel opens with Raka's unwelcome arrival [...]. She is described as having "a pair of extravagantly large and somewhat bulging eyes (39)," and this is another iconographic characteristic of Kali the Crone. In this way her affiliation to the genealogy of wicked women in Kasauli is made explicit.

Besides, Raka shares some common features also with her great-grandmother. They are both skinny, to the point that while embracing each other, "Each felt how bony, angular and unaccommodating the other was and they quickly separated (40)." Similarly, Kali "especially in her early history, is often depicted or described as emaciated, lean, and gaunt." Moreover, to Raka's eyes the interior of Carignano seems like "a blackened, fire- blasted cave in which one fiery, inflamed eye glowed and smouldered by itself (42)." Here the house is described as the obscure forge of the goddess Kali, she who has a third glowing eye, for the great-grandmother is a potential fury, who consumes her passion within herself [...].

Here Raka is represented as bearing vampire-like features, since, rather than becoming pale after hearing the spectral stories about the Pasteur Institute, she seems to partake both physically and naturally with such a place, as Kali the queen of the "cremation ground: where she sits on a corpse surrounded by jackals and goblins [...]. She sits on a corpse in the crematorium ground, and is surrounded by skulls, bones, and female jackals." Raka is fully at ease in the ravine, where there were "splotches of blood, there were yellow stains oozing through paper, there were bones and the mealy ashes of bones (48)" and jackals [...].

Raka is further described as a "perceptive child (46)," always set in motion by an exploratory drive. Insight and lively intuition are also the main characteristics of Kali as shakti, that is of Kali the powerful one [...].

Apart from her ugly appearance, what also strikes Nanda Kaul is her loneliness and total indifference: "But Raka ignored her. She ignored her so calmly, so totally that it made Nanda Kaul breathless. She eyed the child with apprehension now, wondering at this total rejection, so natural, instinctive and effortless when compared with her own planned and willful rejection (47)."

Here Nanda Kaul reveals her inner nature. Her own loneliness and isolation is a pose. It is a mask used in self-defense against a world which has caused her pain and sorrow. In contrast, Raka's solitude is not imposed by external events, it is a natural attitude. And after the physical and behavioural similarities between the two female characters, here Nanda Kaul declares explicitly their affiliation: "Nanda Kaul saw that she was the finished, perfected model of what Nanda Kaul herself was merely a brave, flawed experiment [...] like her own great-grandmother, Raka wanted only one thing—to be left alone (47-48)." Thus the assimilation of the young Raka to the old Crone is here stated explicitly. Raka is the perfected model of her great-grandmother. She has inherited her features and temperament; she is her natural continuation [...].

Raka's lonely roaming is seen as a manifestation of her "genius" or her "daemon (64)" but also as a similarity with her great-grandmother who is ready to admit: "Raka, you really *are* a great-grandchild of mine, aren't you? You are more like me than *any* of my children or grandchildren. You are *exactly* like me, Raka (64)." Moreover, Nanda Kaul also thinks of leaving the Carignano villa to her great-grandchild after her death. In this way, it seems that Raka, too, is assimilated to the mythical figure of Parvati the daughter of the Himalayas, in her quiescent phase, before she reveals her other powers as Kali.

It cannot be pure chance that after receiving the news of her mother's new breakdown, Raka heads for the burnt house on top of the hill, to inspect that vision of destruction. While Carignano is the house that "inscapes the life of Nanda Kaul" and mirrors her self and existence, the burnt house, instead, mirrors Raka's wild nature. This sinister interest of Raka's ("a morbid, psychopathic love for the dark, destructive, mysterious aspects of life") is once more underlined by her assimilation to the crazy goddess Kali: "No one ever came here but Raka and the cuckoos that sang and sang invisibly. These were not the dutiful domestic birds that called Nanda Kaul to attention at Carignano. They were the demented birds that raved and beckoned Raka on to a land where there was no sound, only silence, no light, only shade, and skeletons kept in beds of ash on which the footprints of jackals flowered in grey (90)" [...].

Ila Das is described in the third section of the novel as the victim of the assault of some school-boys, who in the end take her umbrella and crash and kick it till it is stuck among the railings of the fence which runs along the road. If the doomed umbrella taken from Ila Das is on one level a mock-sacrificial object, it also anticipates issues of more violence to come. By the way, significandy, the first section of the novel is entitled "Nanda Kaul at Carignano," the preposition "at" giving a sense of permanence; the second section is entitled "Raka Comes to Carignano," the preposition "to" stressing the arrival without anticipating permanence or departure; while the third is entitled "Ila Das leaves Carignano," as if her arrival was the prelude to her ultimate departure [...]. Ila Das's visit is welcomed exactly as Raka was before her, as an inevitable intruder: "Nanda Kaul looked down from her height, having invited her to tea, having failed to put her away out of sight and mind." (112)

Ila Das had a hard life, though in a different way, made as it is of privations and poverty, nevertheless she still cares for the social problems which continue to plague India. On the contrary, Nanda Kaul has never experienced such an engagement, she smoulders her rage within herself and her retirement. Ila Das still fights against local superstitious priests, who deny the children the possibility to be treated in hospitals, and let them die. Furthermore, Ila Das is conscious of the role of women in the process of modernisation that India is undergoing after Independence: "the women are willing, poor dears, to try and change their dreadful lives by an effort, but do you think their men will let them? Nooo, not one bit (129)." Therefore, Ila Das is aware of the subordinate condition of women, especially evident in the practice of child-marriage, that Indian legislation has abolished and Ila Das is still trying to stop.

Ila Das's final comment on the dry weather and on the risk of forest fires is just an echo of Nanda Kaul's brooding over the lack of water in Kasauli if compared with the richness in lakes and rivers of the Kashmir of her childhood. But that dryness has permeated Nanda Kaul, who is dumb to her friend's request of help, and indifferent to her friend's social involvement to improve life for women. Both Nanda Kaul's recollections of her childhood, spent in lakes and rivers, and Ila Das's umbrella in a dry season and in the evening hours are emblems of a lost womanhood, of a maternal female world, which has been destroyed by males. Nanda Kaul's husband is the cause of her present aridity and selfishness, while Ila Das's good-for-nothing brothers are the cause of her negated womanhood or even motherhood, since she could never marry.

Nanda Kaul's recommendation to her friend not to preach against the priest, and the grainseller's reproach not to go out at night alone are just anticipations of what is going to happen. Ila Das falls victim of the ambush and rage of Preet Singh, who wants to marry his seven-years-old daughter to a widowed man, and does not accept Ila Das's intrusion in that matter. Ila's sacrificial death and rape catches the reader by surprise, as a signal of that blind violence that uncoils in the darker corners of India.

The death of Ila Das is announced as was her arrival: by a phone-call, from the police station. In this sudden and incredible revelation, Nanda Kaul breaks down and becomes conscious of all the lies she has told herself and Raka of a happy life with her father and her husband, who had married her only to cover his life-long relation with a Christian, Miss David: "She did not live here alone by choice—she lived here alone because that was what she was forced to do, reduced to doing (145)." And while the reader is doubtful about Nanda Raul's surviving the bad news, Raka excitedly calls her: "I have set the forest on fire. Look, Nani—look—the forest is on fire (145)."

Because of its shortness, *Fire on the Mountain* is structured like a short story, or rather like a novella, with the climax at its very end. Thus, in the space of four pages, as many critics have noticed, the climax of this novella is consumed in a fire, and Raka has shown her true face as Kali the destroyer.

The fire is an act of will: Raka had gone to the kitchen and had taken a box of matches to set the forest on fire, to stop the two ladies lying about their happy past, to "wipe it all away," to reduce all its stories and violence to silence. Whatever is latent in Nanda Raul, her resentment, her rage and vengeance is patent in Raka. Parvati the spouse, has become Durga the inaccessible, before Raka made her appearance and fully displayed her powers as Kali, the fury emanated by Parvati-Durga. Metaphorically, the full moon has ripened and Raka has consciously set a whole world on fire. In spite of her youth and white complexion, which are the reassuring aspects taken by Gauri, the goddess emerging from Parvati's will to get rid of her black colour, she has inherited the dark and fierce spirit of her great-grandmother, thus appearing in her many facets as the goddess Kali [...].

The whole novel, or novella, is built on the attempt to give central focus to what is marginal. First of all, an old woman, representing the marginalised of society, becomes the main protagonist of the story. Secondary characters like Raka and Ila Das introduce other stories of violence within the main narrative. But Raka is a child herself, and paraphrasing the words of Kinsley, both the old (or dead) woman and the infant have a liminal nature. Neither has a complete social identity. Neither fits neatly or at all into the niches and structures of normal society. Both Nanda Kaul and Raka have been excluded from human relationships. "One who approaches Kali in these roles is awakened to a perception of reality that is difficult to grasp within the confines of the order of dharma and a socialized ego." Thus, the fire also represents this final knowledge and reciprocal recognition. The fact that Raka calls her great-grandmother "Nani" in the last episode and had done so only twice before, is a farther

> proof of a deeper recognition, like the infant who on the battleground cried so desperately in order to attract Kali's attention, and conquered her as a mother. Actually, the novel concludes with a double confession. On the one hand Nanda Kaul confesses she has made up all sorts of fantasies and stories, while Raka confesses she has set those same stories on fire [...]. (Concilio 120-34)

A.K. Vishnu holds that Raka "constitutes the core charm of the novel." He writes:

> In the whole range of Desai's fiction, there is none else like her. An intimate observation of her activities in the novel reveals mysterious dimensions of her personality. If Carignano is an abode of solitaries, the most fitting one amongst them all is Raka. Uptill her arrival Carignano had been having the creditable status of discarding its inhabitants. It is Raka, who, for the first ever time in its history, totally discards it:
>
> Carignano had much to offer—yes, she admitted that readily, nodding her head like a berry—it was the best of places she'd lived in ever. Yet it had in its orderly austerity something she found confining, restricting. It was a dry and clean as a nut but she burst from its shell like an impatient kernel, small and explosive. (91)

Instead of Carignano she is drawn towards a burnt house on the top of another knoll:

> This hill, with its one destroyed house and one unbuilt one, on the ridge under the fire—singed pines, appealed to Raka with the strength of a strong sea-current—pulling, dragging. There was something about it—illegitimate, uncompromising and lawless—that made her tingle. (90)

Raka dislikes being in Carignano. In fact, "Raka no more needed, or wanted, a house than a jackal did, or a cicada. She was a wild creature—wild, wild, wild [...]" (103). Carignano fails to tame her, besiege her like couples of its previous inhabitants [...]" (Vishnu 83-84).

We can conclude this discussion of the characters in the novel with the observation of **Pandey** and **Rao:**

> In all her novels, Anita uses psychology as a dominant discipline in the shaping of character; this, together with

> the formal handling of various literary devices and the attention she pays to the craftsmanship, puts her on a plane quite different from any other Indian English novelist before her.
>
> (*Image of India in the Indian Novel in English* [Eds] Sudhakar Pandey and R. Raja Rao. Bombay. Orient Longman, 1993. p. xvii)

Shiv K. Kumar appears to be unnecessarily harsh in his remark that "wooden sexless characters stalk across her pages, chasing dark shadows at twilight" (*The Twofold Voice* [...] ed. Rizvi. 1982. 191-92).

6

Images and Symbols

Like most modern writers Anita Desai also tries to convey her perception of life or, more precisely, the conditions of her characters and their psychological reactions to the situations they are placed in, through images and symbols. Since the major theme of her novels, including *Fire on the Mountain* is alienation it is only natural that the images and symbols of alienation abound in her novels.

To Magda Costa's question, "how did you become a writer?," Anita Desai replied:

> When I was a very little girl we had a house full of books. All of us were great readers. We were always going to the library and the bookshop. When I was taught how to write and read at school I remember I made up my mind that this was what I'd love to do best and this was the world I was going to occupy. So I started writing little stories in that time. I never really wanted to do anything else. I think it was simply a love of books, and the *pleasure I found in imagining images within words.* [emphasis added]

To Magda's question, "Where do you start from when you think of a novel to write?" Anita Desai said:

> Usually quite a small detail, may be just a single image. That image stays in your mind, so that you keep returning to it, and you keep adding other images to it, which fit, which are suitable and appropriate to it. So that gradually begins to grow.

The author also admits:

> Sometimes an image doesn't grow; it remains where it is and never becomes a story, but sometimes it puts out branches, leaves, fruit, and then becomes a book. We might

as well begin our study of the images and symbols of *Fire on the Mountain* from this premise or angle, and thus see how certain images put out branches and blossom to hold the book together, and send tentacles through the whole of its texture. One such rich and organic image here is 'house.'

House

The following passage from Anita Desai's *Clear Light of Day* illustrates the layered associations that the image of the house can stir in the author's stream of consciousness. "It seemed to her [Bim] that the dullness and the boredom of her childhood, her youth, were stored here in the room under the worn dusty red rugs, in the bloated brassware, amongst the dried grasses in the swollen vases, behind the yellowed photographs in the oval frames—everything, everything that she had so hated as a child and that was still preserved here as if this were the storeroom of some dull, uninviting provincial museum." Again, on another occasion Desai's protagonist is made to realize other dimensions of the 'house.'

> With her inner eye she saw how her own house and its particular history linked and contained her, as well as her whole family [...] giving them the soil in which to send down their root [...] always drawing from the same soil, the same secret darkness. That soil contained all time, past and future [...]. It was where her deepest self lived, and the deepest selves of her sisters and brothers and all those who shared that time with her. *(Clear Light of Day)*

Carignano: A House of Nanda's Own

Several houses have been introduced in the narration— some real, some imaginary—among which Carignano emerges as the most important location in the story. Carignano, Nanda Kaul's hill station house, is structurally pivotal in serving the function of unifying the three parts of the novel, as the subtitles indicate. Carignano has been, furthermore, envisioned and foregrounded as a very special 'space' in both the literal and metaphorical senses.

Carignano, Nanda Kaul's "home on the ridge," is characterized by starkness, and she would not have it otherwise. Like the Kasauli mountain the house too commands a sweeping view.

> The sun shone on its white walls. Its windows were open—the ones facing north opened onto the blue waves of the Himalayas flowing out and up to the line of ice and snow sketched upon the sky, while those that faced south looked down the plunging cliff to the plain stretching out, flat and sere, to the blurred horizon. (4)

At "the topmost height of her garden" there is a knoll, which Nanda Kaul prefers on her solitary roamings,—"the knoll, the topmost height of her garden, where the wind was keenest and the view widest."

Strolling up to the knoll, her favourite spot, Nanda Kaul gazes at "her house" with satisfaction:

> [...] simple and white and shining on the bleached ridge. On the north side the wall was washed by the blue shadows of the low, dense apricot trees. On the east wall, the sun glared, scoured and sharp. It seemed so exactly right a house for her, it satisfied her heart completely. How could it ever have belonged to anyone else? What could it possibly have been like before Nanda Kaul came to it? She could not imagine. (5)

As the novel opens, Nanda Kaul has already arrived at Kasauli, and settled in her hill station house 'Carignano'; and she seems to have found a sort of contentment. She has, as it were, reached a fulfilment of a life-long dream:

> Everything she wanted was here, at Carignano, in Kasauli. Here, on the ridge of the mountain, in this quiet house. It was the place, and the time of life, that she had wanted and prepared for all her life—as she realized on her first day at Carignano, with a great, cool flowering of relief—and at last she had it. She wanted no one and nothing else. Whatever else came, or happened here, would be an unwelcome intrusion and distraction. (3)

In Carignano her own children, the sons and daughters who had come up to help her "empty the Vice-Chancellor's house," and escort her to this hill station residence, do not seem to belong. "For a while, they had stood about, in Carignano, like too much furniture. She had wondered what to do with them." (30)

When they leave at last, she feels relieved. Abandoned and alone, she turns to the house. This is the first time in her life that she can pace 'proprietorially' in a house, all her own:

> When they left, she paced the house, *proprietorially,* feeling the feel of each stone in the paving with bare feet.

Nanda Kaul accepts this house just as it is,—barren, empty, devoid of decorative details. She does not even think of any improvisation. After her escorts leave, and she is left alone in her own house for the first time in her life:

> She had drifted about the garden. Unlike any other owner of house and garden, she had not said: Here I will plant a willow, there I will pull out the Spanish broom and put in pampas grass instead.

Rather, she seems to enjoy the very emptiness, the withered unkempt garden, and the pebbly gravel.

> [...] she reveled in its barrenness, its emptiness. The loose pebbles of the gravel pleased her as much as rich turf might another. She cared not to add another tree to the group of apricots by the veranda or the group of three pines at the gate.

At the opening of Chapter 8 we see Nanda Kaul "seated on the veranda in the late afternoon shade" and reading in small sips, bits and pieces from *The Pillow Book of Sei Shonagon.*

The passage she reads is about a woman living alone in her own house:

> When A Woman Lives Alone was the title of one scrap that caught her eye:
>
> When a woman lives alone, her house should be extremely dilapidated, the mud wall should be falling to pieces, and if there is a pond, it should be overgrown with water plants. It is not essential that the garden be covered with sage-brush, butt weeds should be growing through the sand in patches, for this gives the place a poignantly desolate look.
>
> I greatly dislike a woman's house when it is clear she has scurried about with a knowing look on her face, arranging everything just as it should be, and when the gate is kept tightly shut.
>
> Nanda Kaul looked up with a faint smile, then bent her head to read it over again. Each time it went down her throat with a clear, luminous passage, like a chilled dry wine. (27)

The author attempts to draw a parallel between Nanda Kaul and her garden in Carignano.

> Like her, the garden seemed to have arrived, simply by a process of age, of withering away and an elimination, at a state of elegant perfection. It was made up of a very elements, but they were exact and germane as the strokes in a Japanese scroll. She no more wished to add to them than she wished to add to her own pared, reduced and radiantly single life. (31)

Children imply change and evolution, continued renewal of life. The desire for any of this has withered in Nada. That's why

> She could no more picture a child—in this perfected and natural setting than she could a pergola of roses, a marble faun or a fountain. She wished for none of these. On the contrary, the thought of them sickened as a box of sweets might sicken. (31)

Nanda loves the barrenness of Carignano.

What pleased and satisfied her so, here at Carignano, was its barrenness (4). Even the grass in the garden is "short" and "dry," and the clumps of iris "had finished blooming." And the yellow rose-creeper that the Misses 'Huges' had planted in the past to climb the railing is just "a furry grey mass" all the year, "stirring and rustling as if it housed a colony of mice." But still this creeper would burst in a brief blossom every April.

> In April it would exhale a billowing cloud of pale yellow roses—an extravagance, a flamboyance, a largesse of roses, of creamy yellow, of the scent of damp tea-leaves. Every year Nanda Kaul stared at it in astonishment, wondering where all this lacy, frilly prettiness came from in her hard, stony garden, gale-blown and dour. It crept over the outdoor kitchen, over the woodhouse, and trailed upon every rail, gate and fence, sleeping and sighing all year but for that one month when it was re-born like a sweet, angelic infant in pastel frills and flounces. Then Nanda Kaul stopped to muse upon the Misses Hughes for a while. (8-9)

It is "re-born like an angelic infant" in "her hard, stony garden," and Nanda Kaul cannot altogether ignore its charm. Is it a kind of foreshadowing, that once again she will be charmed by another child?

Although Nanda Kaul cannot imagine any prior owner of the house, the house has a history, which is also related to the history of colonial India. While Nanda Kaul apparently does not know, and is also indifferent to this history, the postman knows only some fragments of it. It is the omniscient author's prerogative to share a glimpse of that history with the reader. She tries to give it a flavour of authenticity by alluding to personal memoirs and adding up imaginative details. The history includes and involves various tales of alienation and unhappiness of aliens as well as sadly comical tales of erratic expatriates. The house seems to have chosen its chain of lonely dwellers,—frequently they were women— sad or eccentric in their own ways.

> [...] it had been built in 1843, by a Colonel Macdougall, for his wife who could not bear the heat in the military cantonment at Ambala in the plains and hoped to save her ominously pale children by taking them to the mountains in the summer. So it says in his memoirs, which he had privately published and distributed but which are no longer available. He ended his account of his active life and the many military manoeuvres in which he had taken part with a description of this house he called Carignano and of how he and his wife Alice would sit by the window of an evening—she wrapped in a cashmere shawl for she was sickly and he with his pipe and tobacco—and gaze out across the valley to Sabathu where, amongst the white flecks of the gravestones in the military cemetery, their own seven children came to be buried, one by one. (6)

Apparently for Colonel Macdougall's Alice, this land of "heat and dust" was no wonderland, promising wonderful things, but rather the burial ground of their dreams and hopes. Eventually they too died here and were buried in the same cemetery down the hills.

The subsequent associations of the house also are not too happy ones. For example there is the grim anecdote about a violent thunderstorm which had nearly ruined the house that "stood empty for some years" after the death of its first owners.

> The entire roof—sheets of corrugated iron that Colonel Macdougall had had painted green but that had eventually faded to its natural rusty grey—was lifted off the square stone walls and hurled down the hill as far as

> Garkhal where its sharp edge sliced the head off a coolie who was trying to shelter beside a load of stacked wood on the roadside.

In a note of grim irony the author adds:

> Eventually the roof was replaced—but not the coolie's head—[...].

After this the house goes to the pastor of the local church. This man fails to make a cottage garden, but succeeds in planting and bringing up three apricot trees, and setting up a bird-bath. But even his small success story is laced with the dressing of the tragedy of others and misery of himself owing to the failure of his marriage. It is, again, a grim tale, though told with the ironical dissociation of a comedy-writer. The pastor, on taking over the house

> [...] found it sad that its exposed situation on the ridge made it impossible to plant the cottage garden he would have liked but he did plant three apricot trees where the house sheltered them from the worst gales, and they flourished in the stony soil and bore fruit. In his delight he bought a marble bird bath at a sale held at the Garden House whose owners, the aged sisters Abbott, died within a week of each other and whose goods were auctioned off, and placed it under the trees. It was his joy to watch the bulbuls and hoopoes come to feast on the apricots and flutter down into the bird bath and plunge and preen and scatter the water in spray. (6-7)

But this is only a very feeble and brief respite in a life which is otherwise one of prolonged ordeal. It is no less sad for being macabre.

> His joy would have been complete if his wife had made him apricot jam. But she would not. She hated him too much to cook jam for him. The longer their marriage the more she hated him and almost daily she made an attempt to murder him. But he survived. When she had her back turned he would pour out the tea she had brewed for him into a pot of geranium and silently watch them droop and die. He woke to see her the second before she plunged the kitchen knife into him and learnt to sleep with one eye open till he went blind—but that was after Mavis died: slipping on her way to the outdoor kitchen, she plunged

> down the cliff and spilt her head open on a rock, and so he lived on safely and died 'peacefully,' as they say, in a bed in Lady Linlithgow's sanatorium for the tubercular.

After this the house earns the reputation of being a 'haunted' house visited by the ghost of the unhappy man now dead.

> His ghost was said to haunt the house, or at least his pipe did, for a certain moment of the evening the veranda would be wafted over by the rich, ripe odour of invisible tobacco freshly kindled. (7)

The next occupant of the house, however, was not to be daunted by the ghost, but she was disgusted by the lowly taste of the ghost regarding his tobacco. This unmarried lady, who had been governess in an aristocratic household in England, had come over to India after her retirement, in order to avoid the English climate. Here we have a fine humorous touch about a living human reacting to a ghost. Miss Appleby, we are told, "certainly smelt the tobacco. [And] Being used to the finest cheroot in the fine Stuart household [where she worked], it would make her jump up and stamp her foot and yell with rage. The worst was that the ghost himself never appeared or Miss Appleby would surely have flung her entire willow pattern dinner set at him."

Miss Appleby was an eccentric woman known for her 'temper.' Absurd stories naturally sprang up around such personalities, stories meant for local consumption. For example,

> She once thrashed the gardener for planting marigolds which she hated—[...] but climbed onto his back and whipped him around the garden, yelling 'No marigolds, understand? No marigolds in my garden!'

Miss Appleby and the subsequent female owners of the house represent a typical imperial pattern of life and ownership in the colonial hill station.

> She (Miss Appleby) was the first in the long line of maiden ladies who inhabited Carignano—all English of course for in those days all the houses along the Mall were owned by English people and Indians were not so much as allowed to walk on the Mall but were expected to keep to the footpaths on the hillsides and respectfully cast their eyes down when the English sahibs and memsahibs cantered by on their horses.

No wonders the natives, pushed back to the margin or 'footpath,' spin yarns of 'legends' about these 'good women,' as part of the poor man's carnival.

> There was a legend attached to each of these maiden ladies and the postman knew a few of them.

These legends included one Miss Lawrence, who had ridden across the desert of Thar in Rajasthan in linen hat and veil, while assuming it was the Sahara, the two Misses Hughes (called Huges by the people, perhaps for their physical build), who were obsessive housekeepers with their jam-making and china-fixing ventures, and tried to add some gaudy touch to the otherwise dull house, and plant a yellow rose creeper to climb the railing of the house. The Hughes sisters were followed by Miss Jane Shrewsbury who claimed to be a quack and was the subject of a notorious scandal.

> Miss Jane Shrewsbury brewed a more notorious stuff out of the things she grew or dug out of this garden—she said it cured scorpion bites and claimed to have saved many a stung villager carried up to her house, howling in agony. She also poked a fork into her cook's neck when he was choking on a mutton bone in the belief it would make an aperture for him to breathe through. Unfortunately he died and there was much scandal before Dr. Hardy, the local medical lion, gave out that it was definitely the mutton bone that killed him and not the fork as suggested by the local scandalmongers.

Subsequent to Miss Jane's own death here two years later, the war broke out. During the war years two gay ladies took over the house and entertained the 'Tommies' to drink parties. Then suddenly the past came to an end. The author sums up the historical process of transit, along with its binarial implications at social-personal levels, with fine ironical touches:

> Suddenly it was all over. It was 1947. Maiden ladies were not thought to be safe here any more. Quickly, quickly, before the fateful declaration of independence, they were packed onto the last boats and shipped back to England—virginity intact, honour saved, natives kept at bay. A hefty sigh went up—of relief, of regret. A commonplace remark amongst them had been how like Kasauli was to English country towns of memory. Back in those English

> country towns, so unexpectedly and prematurely, they sighed and said no, these were nothing like Kasauli, let alone Simla. But there was nothing to be done, no going back. Carignano was up for sale and Nanda Kaul bought it. The little town went native. (9-10)

Thus in the brief history of the house, which replicates and forms part of the history of the hill station itself, we have in a nutshell a fine picture of a section of the British expatriates in India over a historical period of a century,—their power, whims and ways during the heyday of colonialism,—encapsulated within the history of Carignano. It is a history told with humour, with an occasional touch of irony, but without a tinge of malice.

Nanda Kaul's freedom is also seen to coincide—perhaps incidentally though—with the freedom of India.

Carmen Concilio, however, reads some other feminist meanings, and supposedly 'Indian' significances in the projection of Carignano as an image. As Concilio puts it:

> Carignano was first inhabited by a married couple with children and then by a "long line of maiden ladies (8)," all English, before a native, Nanda Kaul, came there after the declaration of independence. Thus the house itself might be seen as the temple of the trinitarian Goddess, as it was inhabited by the Maiden, the Mother and, eventually, by the Crone. Yet, if the house is a temple, then it is the residence of the two terrible goddesses who respectively represent the intermediate and final emanation of Parvati, namely Durga and Kali, since in the past all the male inhabitants of the house risked or underwent violent deaths.
>
> The married couple lost their seven children there, and when the roof of the house was hurled down by a storm it caused the death of a coolie. Apparently, many of the women living there manifested violent attitudes. One almost killed her husband with a knife, and it is said that his ghost still haunts the house; another was famous for her temper and she reported to have "climbed onto his [her gardener's] back and whipped him around the garden, yelling 'No marigolds, understand?' [...] (8)"; another used to grow strange herbs which were supposed to cure scorpion bites, and once she killed her cook with a

> fork, in the attempt to save him from choking. This line of women also seem to share some of the characteristics often attributed to Kali, the terrible Crone: a violent attitude, magic and obscure powers as administrators of death on their consorts (Kali is portrayed as usually standing or dancing on Shiva's prone or dead body). Therefore, if the house is a temple at all, it is a temple devoted to rituals of domestic and uncouth violence. (Concilio 15-16)

Carignano: Inheritor

At one point, after Raka has come and settled down in Carignano, like an "uninvited mouse or cricket," Nanda Kaul wonders:

> Would she own it herself one day, Carignano? [...] Ought she to leave it to Raka? Certainly it belonged to no one else. Raka alone understood Carignano, knew what Carignano stood for—she alone valued that. Nanda Kaul knew. (80)

During these days she occasionally even thinks of making a will to leave the legal ownership of the house to Raka.

> She thought of making a will. The thought was distasteful. It meant asking the lawyer over and she wished no one to come. She wished no one to go either—certainly not Raka. (80)

Of course she also feels that Raka does not perhaps require a house at all; the child seems to be more like a rabbit or insect burrowing into the hills. So Nanda Kaul also considers the alternative of leaving the house to Raka's mother instead, who, she apprehends, may require a house Or shelter of her own sooner or later.

In connection with this issue of choosing an inheritor for a house, and 'to' a house, one is reminded of E.M. Forster's *Howard's End.* In Forster's novel Ruth Wilcox, an aged lady, and proprietor of the country house named 'Howard's End,' wants to choose a right inheritor to the house on the eve of her death; because Ruth feels the house has a spirit of its own, and if people tried to possess it mechanically, just as some tangible property, they would fail to inherit it. In *Howard's End* the story evolves around precisely this question: who would be, and should be, inheriting the house. In *Fire on the Mountain* the issue of inheritance is of course not the main focus. Nevertheless, like Howard's End, Carignano too—both are small houses, not important as architecture, or denoting power/wealth/comfort—draws together a number of motifs and has been made to play an important structural and thematic role. Nanda Kaul, with her aristocracy of emotions, and Raka, with her unpretentious instinctive response, are in harmony with the 'spirit' or the 'inscape' of the house.

Other Houses on the Hills: the Burnt House

Besides Carignano there are some other houses on the hill, including one which has been burnt down and another which has been left unfinished; there is also the description of some imaginary houses which serve as either extensions or counterpoints to Carignano.

> At the top of the hill there is a burnt house.
>
> It was only the charred shell of a small stone cottage. The veranda roof was already torn off and flung onto the hillside, the paving stones of the floor were cracked and gaping. The doors swung open, the window-frames hung askew, shattered glass lay amongst the cinders. The stairs were a tumble of rocks and weeds. (90)

The rooms are "scorched, empty," "the sagging roof [...] dipped lower every day," and all-around there is the "murmuring, sickening silence" (90), which is only further accentuated by the sudden cooing of the wild mad bird 'from nowhere.'

One is struck by the resemblance between this passage and the following lines from *The Waste Land*:

> In this decayed hole among the mountains [...]
>
> Over the tumbled graves [...]
>
> There is the empty chapel, only the wind's home.
>
> It has no windows, and the door swings.
>
> Dry bones can harm no one.
>
> Only a cock stood on the rooftree.
>
> Co co rico co co rico. (11. 385-92)

The house seems to hold an irresistible attraction for Raka.

Other Houses on the Hills: the Unbuilt House

Raka is also drawn by an unbuilt house on another knoll. The fire which had burnt the cottage mentioned above, had scared away another prospective builder.

> Further up the ridge, on another knoll, was a house for which stones had been bought and heaped but which had

> never been built, so that they lay stacked under the wind-stripped pines, lichen creeping over them like a shroud. It was said that the owners of the land had been frightened off by the forest fire that had razed the small cottage and so abandoned the building of it. (90)

The unfinished house seems to belong to another world, to 'death's dream kingdom.' Even the birds that haunted the abandoned building are different are demented; and they "raved and beckoned Raka on to a land where there was no sound, only silence, no light, only shade, and skeletons kept in beds of ash on which the footprints of jackals flowered in grey" (90).

Dream Houses

As Nanda Kaul tells Raka stories which are supposed to be of her own past she also gives her pictures of imaginary houses. The most fantastic of these houses is the one of her childhood in Kashmir. It is a house encircled by a Paradisiac garden with apple orchards, plums and peaches, almonds and walnuts, pistachios and chilgoza, apricots and raisins. The house contained a private zoo. "Oh, the house in Kashmir was full, full of animals, the strangest ones," as Nanda tells Raka, including a great Himalayan bear, and leopard cats, and lorises, and a pangolin.

In order to impress Raka Nanda Kaul conjures up a 'wonderland' or Disneyland while attempting to describe a plausible yet attractive house. She proudly emphasizes:

> We had a proper house, on the banks of the Dal Lake.

And then dreamily continues to draw the peripheries of the house:

> There was a stream, you know at the back of the house, lined with poplars and willows [...]. In the rains, the stream would fill and sometimes overflow into the garden so that the back door opened into a lake [...].
>
> All round the house was an orchard. Mostly apple trees [...]. There were almonds [...] walnut trees (...) *gucchi,* those curly black dried mushrooms, [...] apricots and raisins. (93-94)

When describing/inventing the interior of the house Nanda Kaul introduces as fascinating an item as a 'private zoo,' since her father's favourite hobby was collecting animals. Nanda Kaul exclaims:

> Oh, the house in Kashmir was full, full of animals, the strangest ones. He had a bear, you know, a great big Himalayan bear that he had found as a cub in the forest There it lived, in our house, in a cage, like a pet King Kong. (95)

One must admit Nanda Kaul is a really imaginative storyteller as she adds up bits and strokes and builds the wonderland extempore. At the same time, it may also be noted that her dream house is a bit different from the Disneylands or from Alice's wonderland. It contains the possibilities of a quite different kind, of violence and 'massacre,' what with its fierce dogs and the terrifying lot of fish-devouring caged leopards. As she adds: also there were "hunting dogs, big wild mastiffs [which] could not stand the sight or smell of bear" and "would have to be locked upstairs whenever the bear was let out," because otherwise "there would have been a massacre."

Nanda Kaul's paternal house, as she claims, contained even wilder and smellier creatures than the bear.

> We had a cage of leopard cats. [...] My father kept them on the landing, just outside his room, and whenever anybody came near, they'd spit and snarl. Even he could not touch without the leather gloves. [...] We used to catch fish in the stream for them, but we never dared feed them ourselves—they had such sudden, vicious claws. (96)

Nanda Kaul also adds some brighter, radiant, or softer touches to this picture of her father's Kashmiri garden house. It is, as the author slyly remarks, like some "slide-show, coloured and erratic" (96).

> Then there were the peacocks in the garden, Raka, and perhaps they were the only tame creatures we had—nearly tame. You wouldn't have thought so when you heard them screaming like wild things in the orchard, but if they saw us having our meals out on the terrace, in summertime, they would come at a run and peck the rice off our plates, greedily. [...] We enjoyed sharing our meals with the peacocks [...].
>
> And [...] the lorises [...] slept all day and you had to stay up at night if you wanted to play with them. They were like babies, the way they'd cling to your arm or neck, and their huge, round eyes would shine in the dark as they

> moved slowly, slowly about the room [...]. Oh yes, all my father's animals lived inside [...]. (96-97)

The house of Nanda Kaul's husband is also described by her in a similar vein. The house was surrounded by open fields for miles where the loving father, Raka is told, would go riding with his children. This house too harboured pets, including dogs, cats, monkeys and horses.

The interior of her husband's house is made to appear as one of dazzling splendour:

> The house I had in the plains was crowded, too crowded —my parents' things, my husband's things, his family's. There were Persian carpets his father had bought in Iran when he was with the Ambassador there. There was glass his mother had bought in Venice. There were the Moghul miniatures my husband collected. (86)

The narration about this idyllic house is, however, concluded with the information that the house had been 'given up' to the next Vice-Chancellor, and the wonderful collection had been distributed among Nanda Kaul's children.

When Ila Das comes to visit Carignano she adds her own splash of gaudy colour to the picture Nanda Kaul has already drawn of the Vice-Chancellor's house. In her characteristic tone of loud enthusiasm she hammers on:

> [...] Oh, the Vice-Chancellor's house—[...] that home away from home for me. All the old customs, the old ways, they got a new lease of life in the Vice-Chancellor's house [...]. The last of the gracious old homes [...]. (119)

Ila Das paints her fabulous picture of the welcoming home:

> [...] tea waiting in winter, lemonade in the summer—pets running free everywhere, the children and their friends playing cricket on the lawn, and all cares could be forgotten for an evening. (121)

She would enumerate the pleasures and joys in that house.

> In winter, we'd stay indoors and there'd be music. [...] The piano, the flute, the veena, the sitar—and so many voices singing, in so many languages. Those are memories to treasure [...]. And your great-grandmother always a picture. No matter how simple the occasion, she was always in silk, always in pearls and emeralds [...]. (121)

There are also references to the houses of Nanda's 'collector' sisters:

> [...] my sisters were all collectors—in their homes you would see *tankhas,* human hip-bone trumpets, carpets and furs [...]. (85)

There are also images suggesting the replication of a house. For example, the 'houseboats' mentioned in Nanda's story of her Kashmiri childhood. Nanda Kaul's reminiscences about the house of her childhood also include images suggesting miniature houses or house-like items; for instance, houseboats or even walnut trees huge as a house. She tells Raka:

> In summer, yes, we did take a houseboat, or sometimes two, and them punted to Nagin Lake. (92)

Also the three huge walnut trees in the imaginary garden of the imaginary Kashmir house:

> There were [...] three walnut trees (in the garden surrounding the house)—each one was as big as a house— yes, each was bigger than Carignano, a house of branches and leaves—and we would get sackfuls of nuts from them. (94)

Significantly Nanda Kaul leaves Carignano untouched as she goes on weaving fantasies around the other houses of her past. Those were houses of others, her father's house, her husband's house. Carignano is the only house which has offered her 'a room of one's own' (a *la* Virginia Woolf). Carignano, the only house which has been Nanda's own, therefore, in its bareness, silence and peace, stands out as a counterpoint to all the other houses, built upon traditional paradigms of grand houses ruled by grand males.

Thus, even during the storytelling period Nanda Kaul ponders one lonely evening:

> She thought of how she had filled, not this house but the other, earlier ones, for Raka's amusement—with furniture, treasures, trophies, even, dear God, with a zoo. She shriveled up in her chair with horror at the thought and relaxed only when she recalled, with dignity, that she had not done that to Carignano. Even when at her most desperate to beguile Raka, she had not used, or misused, Carignano, for that shameful purpose. Carignano she had kept clean, true, open for the wind to blow through. (104)

At the same time, Carignano, the only house of Nanda Kaul's own, bare and clean and silent as it is, offers a point of contrast to the real houses of her past as well in terms of space and privacy and peace.

Real Houses of the Past

The dream houses, constructed by the fantasizing imagination of Nanda Kaul during her 'memory-making' sessions serve to highlight by means of contrast the bareness, the barrenness of the reality. The former are shattered by the assault of the latter on Nanda's consciousness which is stirred into feverish pitch of activity and self-recognition by the message of Ila's death.

About the real houses of Nanda Kaul's past we have hints all along, but at the end there are unambiguous statements. Her father had never been to Tibet, and there was no collection of an explorer to decorate the house; the Buddha was bought from a pedlar. "They had not had bears and leopards in their home, nothing but overfed dogs and bad-tempered parrots" (145).

At one time—the busiest time of her life—it was "the Vice-Chancellor's house." She remembers it as a site for hard mechanical futile and endless work and responsibility that involved the exhausting tasks of childbearing, childrearing, and housekeeping.

> Mentally she stalked through the rooms of that house—*his house, never hers*—very carefully closing the wire-screen doors behind her to keep out the flies, looking sharply to see if the dark furniture, all rosewood, had been polished and the doors of the gigantic cupboards properly shut. She sniffed to make sure the cook was not smoking *biris* in the kitchen and to verify that all the metalware smelt of Brasso. (18; emphasis added)

After spending her best energy and long years of unflagging caring there, she had left it. The children she had borne and reared had come to help her

> empty the Vice-Chancellor's house, pack and crate their belongings and distribute them, then escort her to Kasauli. (30)

After the remembrance and recognition of such knowledge the story-making of Nanda Kaul as well as her own story are bound to come to a halt. So with the vision of the real houses surfacing up in Nanda's consciousness the novel appropriately comes to its end.

It is perhaps natural that whereas the dream houses are drawn elaborately, with eye to minute details, the real houses are mentioned summarily with just a few brush strokes, bold, strong and merciless in their harsh honesty.

Housework: the Sisyphean Task

In the real houses of the past Nanda Kaul had never been the proprietor, but the housekeeper. In this context one is reminded of Simone de Beauvoir's observations in *The Second Sex* on the futility of the task of housekeeping, often keeping houses of others, and the waste it involves for a woman over the years:

> In domestic work, with or without the aid of servants, woman makes her home her own, finds social justification, and provides herself with an occupation, an activity, that deals usefully and satisfyingly with material objects—shining stoves, fresh, clean clothes, bright copper, polished furniture—but provides no escape from immanence and little affirmation of individuality. Such work has a negative basis: cleaning is getting rid of dirt, tidying up is elimination of disorder [...]. Legions of women have only this endless struggle without victory over the dirt. And for even the most privileged the victory is never final.
>
> Few tasks are more like the torture of Sisyphus than house-work, with its endless repetition: the clean becomes soiled, the soiled is made clean, over and over, day after day. The housewife wears herself out marking time: she makes nothing, simply perpetuates the present. She never senses conquest of a positive Good, but rather indefinite struggle against negative Evil. A young pupil writes in her essay: 'I shall never have house-cleaning day'; she thinks of the future as constant progress towards some unknown summit; but one day, as her mother washes the dishes, it comes over her that both of them will be bound to such rites until death. Eating, sleeping, cleaning —the years no longer rise up towards heaven, they lie spread out ahead, grey and identical. The battle against dust and dirt is never won. (470)

Again, in another context, Beauvoir highlights the sad waste involved in meticulous housekeeping:

> She [the woman] can never find salvation in her work itself; it keeps her busy but it does not justify her existence; she lacks the means requisite for self-affirmation as an individual; and in consequence her individuality is not given recognition. Among the Arabs and the Indians and in so many rural populations a woman is only a female domesticated animal, esteemed according to the work she does and replaced without regret if she disappears. In modern civilization she is more or less individualized in her husband's eyes; but unless she completely renounces her ego, engulfing herself [...] in a passionate and tyrannical devotion to her family, she suffers from being reduced to pure generality. She is *the* housekeeper, *the* wife, *the* mother, unique and undiscriminated [...]. (541-42)

These two observations of Beauvoir cited above can help us to see Nanda Kaul's years spent in looking after the 'houses' of others, and her subsequent bitterness and frustration in perspective. The absolute meaninglessness, futility, 'nothing'-ness of the call of housework is also foregrounded in Desai's *In Custody.* Both Deven and his wife are defeated and frustrated in life; but Sarla is necessarily the worse victim, because

> At least Deven had his poetry; *she had nothing,* and so there was an added accusation and bitterness in her look. [emphasis added]

The extreme futility of this meaningless and endless wearying task, which is imposed upon the housewife as some sanctimonious duty, is highlighted in Desai's *Voices in the City.*

> Lives spent in waiting for nothing, waiting on men self-centred and indifferent and hungry and demanding and critical, waiting for death and dying misunderstood, always behind bars that shut us in, in the old houses, in the old city [...].

As Nanda Kaul at Carignano looks back to 'one day in the life of Nanda Kaul in the past, it seems to have been made up of endless drudgery without the respite of silence or peace, and devoid of the privacy of 'a room of one's own.' She thinks of 'all those years' as some 'cluttered, choked' gorge, where countless calls of duty restlessly surged and clamoured about her.

> She thought of the veranda of their house in the [...] Vice-Chancellor's house [...]. She had sat there, not still and emptily, but mending clothes, sewing on strings and buttons and letting out hems, at her feet a small charcoal brazier on which a pot of *kheer* bubbled, snipping threads and instructing the servant girl to stir, stir, don't stop stirring or it'll burn, and then someone had to be called to hold the smallest child from falling into the bubbling pot and carry it away, screaming worse than if it were scalded. Into this din, a tonga had driven up and disgorged a flurry of guests [...] they sat in a ring about her—the wives and daughters of the lecturers and professors over who her husband ruled. She thought of that hubbub and of how she had managed and how everyone had said, [...] 'Really, Vice-Chancellor is lucky to have a wife who can ran everything as she does,' and her eyes flashed when she heard, like a pair of black blades, wanting to cut them, despising them [...]. (18)

As Nanda Kaul mentally revisits the rooms of that house, "his house, never hers," she recaptures it in terms of the daily chores which used to tie her down to that house:

> [...] very carefully closing the wire-screen doors behind her to keep out the flies, looking sharply to see if the dark furniture, all rosewood, had been polished and the doors of the gigantic cupboards properly shut. She sniffed to make sure the cook was not smoking *biris* in the kitchen and to verify that all the metalware smelt freshly of brasso. (18)

Caring for everybody was her responsibility. But was it a joy, even caring for children? Or was it just endless backbreaking duty? As she looks back to those days

> She seemed to hear poignant shrieks from the canna beds in the garden—a child had tumbled off the swing, another had been stung by a wasp, a third slapped by the fourth—and gone out on the veranda to see them come wailing up the steps with cut lips, bruised knees, broken teeth and tears, and bent over the with that still, ironic bow to duty that no one had noticed or defined. (18-19)

The myth of the so-called 'joy of motherhood' has been exploded by feminist writers and thinkers (Buchi Emecheta, for example). Margaret Rivka Polatnick, the sociologist thinker, points out how convention places the burden of parenting exclusively on the women and thus childrearing carries a high price for women in terms of arrested career advancements and lower social status.

> Childrearing [...] is not a source of money, status, power in the society, or power in the family [...]. There are also drawbacks inherent in the nature of the work itself. The rearing of children 'involves long years of exacting labor and self-sacrifice.' (Polatnick 578)

The responsibilities of a childrearer/homemaker are, indeed, not confined to some 40 hours per week. For a married woman with small children it can be as long as 80 hours a week if not more. And "in addition to the actual hours of work, there is the constant strain of being 'on call' " (Polatnick 578), whereas:

> Fathers, with full social support, can buy a significant degree of freedom from direct family responsibility. They have a category of people at hand—women—constrained by social forces to accept that responsibility. Women have no such convenient group to whom they can pass the childrearing buck. For mothers, the price of escape from childrearing—financial, social, psychological—is usually too high. (Polatnick 579)

Leta S. Hollingworth relates the issue to the cultural frame of patriarchal ideology:

> [...] the drudgery, the monotonous labor, and other disagreeable features of childrearing are idealized by "the social guardians." On the other hand, the joys and compensations of motherhood are magnified and presented to consciousness on every hand. Thus the tendency is to create an illusion whereby motherhood will appear to consist of compensations only, and thus come to be desired by those for whom the illusion is intended. (Hollingsworth 20-21)

Nanda's experience of motherhood and wifehood only serves to explode the traditionally celebrated myths about the 'venerated' roles of a woman as mother and wife-cum-housekeeper. The memory of bearing and rearing the many children thus brings no solace to her. It only brings back the feeling of the great discomfort, and the annoyance and botheration she had to bear with during these occasions. And all the time, with so much to do regarding the supervision of the daily household chores, in addition to the huge quantity of washing and ironing, she had to keep up appearances as the proud possession or show-piece in the house,—as the elegant wife of the vice-chancellor.

> [...] there was such a deal of washing and ironing to do and Mr. Kaul had wanted her always in silk, at the head of the long rosewood table in the dining-room, entertaining his guests. (18)

The memory stirs only bitterness or emptiness in her.

Image: Badminton Court

We come to learn about the reality of Nanda's life only at the end. But earlier in the narration we get some suggestive hints. One such hint is made through the image of the badminton court. The badminton court is literally a space, well-defined, bordered, chalked out, clear-cut, measured. At the same time, it becomes a metaphor for the limited, measured out, fixated life of Nanda Kaul as the wife of a successful man, the mother of his children, the perfect hostess, the beautiful possession of a man, but daily trampled for infinite times by the players who control the space.

Years later, in the afternoons in her mountain house, Nanda Kaul would sometimes remember the badminton court in her husband's house. It is not herself as a player that she remembers. The past floats down to her as the memory of one evening when, after people had finished their play, she alone had been pacing in the abandoned court:

> [...] she stepped onto the crisp grass of the lawn [...] almost walking into the badminton net that hung so grey and spidery as to be invisible in the ghostly light. Stepping back, she had walked around the badminton pole, along the line of lime dribbled over the close, dry grass, and stepped over a broken shuttlecock discarded beside a bed of white petunias [...].
>
> There had been badminton earlier in the day—not the children, but teachers, friends from the campus, had come to play. Now they had gone. The court was deserted. A waxen moon was climbing [...]. There was a mixed odour of grass, of phlox, of eucalyptus trees along with lime,

> sweat-soaked sports clothes, catgut and clammy tennis shoes. She sniffed at it with pinched nostrils, finding it offensive, lacking in composition and harmony.
>
> Walking faster and faster back and forth, back and forth over the lawn, she had stayed out till she heard the car [...] her husband [...] had been to drop some of the guests home—no, she corrected herself with asperity, *one* of the guests home. (25)

She silently watched him from her shade going up to his room, and stayed on alone.

> Then she paced the lawn again, slower and slower [...]. She relished the sensation of being alone again. (26)

Is it her attempt to recover the space lost during day time, the space appropriated by her husband, his girlfriend, and all the other appropriators?

However, during her story-telling sessions Nanda Kaul would mention the badminton court with other implications; she mentions it as an evidence in support of the myth of the charming father that her husband was to her children.

> Another thing he got up for the children was a badminton court, and we'd have such games out on the lawn, all of us, at times even by moonlight. (100)

The badminton court figures again dining the 'memory-making' game which Ila Das takes over from Nanda during her visit to Carignano. Ila goes ecstatic as she fantasizes the memory of the past for Raka's consumption, and describes the delightful summer evenings in the Vice-Chancellor's house in those grand old days.

> And after the heat of the day, the lovely evenings out on the freshly watered lawn [...] and the badminton court. How all the teachers waited for an invitation to play badminton at the Vice-Chancellor's house. He used to organize matches, you know—your great-grandfather, my dear. We'd play mixed doubles. I remember playing with one of your great-uncles, my dear, against the Vice-Chancellor and Miss David. Miss David was an *ace* player—ooh, she was good—and they beat us hollow [...].
>
> But the line was cut suddenly as a thread is cut-snip-completely. She was silent. [...] What sharp, swift scissors had descended on that endless tangle of her game? The

> badminton court—mixed doubles—Miss David—and here were Ila Das and Nanda Kaul, both beaten, silent. (121-22)

Thus the badminton court emerges as an image which is symptomatic of Nanda's mangled and trodden life in the Vice-Chancellor's 'house,' *his* space, under *his* authority, at his pleasure.

Image: Text

"Text" as a concept has been variously dealt with by writers and critics of our times. According to Abrams [A *Glossary of Literary Terms* 284-85]:

> Traditional critics have conceived the object of their critical concern to be a literary "work," whose form is achieved by its author's deliberate design and its meanings by the author's intentional uses of the verbal medium. French *structuralist* critics, on the other hand, depersonalized a literary product by conceiving it to be not a "work," but a "text," one species of the social institution called denture (writing). The author is regarded as an impersonal agency in whom the action of writing precipitates aspects of the pre-existing linguistic and literary system into a particular text.

According to Murfin and Ray *[The Bedford Glossary of Critical and Literary Terms 398]:*

> French structuralist critics took issue with the traditional view of literary compositions as "works" [...]. These critics argued that literary compositions are texts rather than works, texts being the product of a social institution they called *écriture* (writing).

Desai here uses the image of the 'text' in its varied forms. As the act of fictionalizing becomes a pivotal factor in the thematic and structural design of the novel, the author's use of the image of 'Text' seems to acquire a special significance to the perceptive reader.

Text: Japanese Scroll

The garden of Carignano, sparse and austere as it is, is accepted by Nada as "a Japanese scroll."

> It was made up of a very few elements, but they were exact and germane as the strokes of a Japanese scroll.

Thus, the garden itself is envisioned as a text, which is sparse yet pleasing to the taste of Nanda Kaul. She finds it adequate, appropriate and acceptable as part of her sparse house on the ridge.

Text: Ancient Scroll

The rain washed mountain scene spreads under Raka's feet like an "an ancient scroll" unrolled. Once she has reached the hilltop, the little girl has an aerial view of the vast scene lying below. The other hills look

> (...) as low and soft as banks of golden moss far below. To the south the plain stretched endlessly out and away, no longer hot and livid under the summer sun but calm and still and cat-grey in the dusk, raked by the shining flow of Punjab's five rivers and Chandigarh's lake set in its breast like a dull silver brooch—not set so much as floating a little above the flatness, suspended in the dusk. There was a breadth of space, a vast, sweeping depth to the scene. Raka thought it like *an ancient scroll* unrolled at her feet for her to survey.
>
> To the north, the soft, downy hills flowed, wave upon wave, gold and blue and violet and indigo, like the sea. (61)

Raka, being a mere child, is not supposed to have the expertise of deciphering an ancient scroll. Such a thing can only tease and tingle her imagination, and we know she is an imaginative child. She can only watch and survey the vast scroll, and get enraptured by its grandeur and mystery. Again, the mountains are 'ancient,' and the anciency further contributes to their mystery. The 'scroll' is a visual narrative; it is an image as well as a message/or narrative/ or story. Thus, the mountain itself is envisioned as a text, albeit a mysterious one, which is supposed hide undecipherable meanings behind its hieroglyphics of rocks and stones, pines and cicadas, eagles and vultures, as well as miles and miles of multilayered waves of light and colour, wind and rain.

The metaphor of 'ancient scroll' brings out Raka's sense of awe at the mystery and profundity of the mountain-scape. It is to her a beautiful, mysterious, inscrutable, yet profoundly mysterious and endlessly fascinating text.

Text: The Memoir of the Colonel

In contrast to the 'text's which serve as metaphor for nature,—garden or mountain—there is another kind of texts introduced in this novel. Compared to the former category, these are much narrower and necessarily limited ones, because firstly these are created by some human agents, and secondly these are conditioned by the respective writers' immediate social-historical circumstances.

Colonel Macdougall, a British official in India, carrying the 'white man's burden' on his shoulders, had built Carignano in 1843, that is the early days of British colonialism in India, and had written his memoirs, "which he had privately published and distributed but which are no longer available" (6). In these memoirs he put on record that Carignano was built by him "for his wife who could not bear the heat in the military cantonment at Ambala in the plains and hoped to save her ominously pale children by taking them to the mountains in the summer" (6). The author notes with a tinge of sympathetic flavour:

> He ended his account of his active life and the military manoeuvres in which he had taken part with a description of this house he called Carignano and of how he and his wife Alice would sit by the window of an evening— she wrapped in a cashmere shawl for she was sickly and he with his pipe and tobacco—and gaze out across the valley to Sabathu where, amongst the white flocks of the gravestones in the military cemetery, their own seven children came to be buried, one by one. (6)

This is the imperial text, scribed once, but now erased by the process of time which operates through the great erasures of nature and history. In a way, this is also a story of an exile, lost to the margins of an empire. His act of building the house and his act of writing the memoirs can be thus seen as part of a broader pattern of history,—the desperate, pathetic and slightly ironical history of the colonial exiles, the twentieth century versions of Shelley's 'Ozymandias.' After all a text which was meant to be of glory and appropriation, eventually ends in sadness and desolation.

Past as a Text

Nanda Kaul remembers her own past itself as a 'book,' which was disorderly and crowded with unnecessary details. The act of remembering personal ordeals in terms of a 'book' shows her effort to reach a sort of 'dissociation of sensibility.'

> She had suffered from the nimiety, the disorder, the fluctuating and unpredictable excess.
>
> She had been so glad when it was over. She had been glad to leave it all behind, in the plains, like a great, heavy, difficult book that she had read through and was not required to read again.
>
> Would Raka's coming mean the opening of that old, troublesome ledger again? (30)

Nanda Kaul's obvious dissatisfaction with this 'book' or text that had been imposed on her by life and society may account for her invention of a new text down memory lane, which she paints with the added colours and contours of fantasy in order to make a lovely and attractive text, however unreal it might be.

Text: Memory-making

Nanda Kaul engages in an act of memory-making, which is also a way of creating a text. At a later stage in the narrative Ila Das enters the scene to join this game of 'memory-making.' But what is produced in course of this game turns out to be a fragile text. At the mention of Miss David 'beating' them hollow in the badminton game, the flow is snapped, "the line was cut [...] completely." Suddenly "speech had been snatched out [...] and whisked away." The endless tangles of the text have been, as it were, suddenly snipped off by some "sharp, swift scissors."

Asha's Letter as a Text

Asha's letter to her mother is also a text. It is the insensitive text of a patriarchal ideology, absorbed and internalized by a so-called modern woman. It is perhaps understandable that Nanda Kaul, who has received similar letters from Asha earlier, feels "an enormous reluctance" to open this letter.

> She looked at it with distaste and foreboding for a long time before she finally tore it open and drew out the bundle of dark blue pages across which Asha's large writing pranced. This writing had none of the writer's loveliness—it sprawled and spread and shrieked out loud an aggressive assurance and aplomb. (14)

The text contained within this "aggressive" script is also equally appropriately insentient and cruel. Asha, in spite of being a mother, buys and sells off the patriarchal dictum that making a home is entirely the woman's responsibility, and the question of dignity or decency simply does not arise. As she writes to Nanda Kaul,

> [...] he [Tara's husband] is not really so bad as Tara might make you believe, she simply does not understand him, doesn't understand *men,* and she really is the wrong type of wife for a man like him so I can't blame him *entirely* although it is true that he does drink [...]. (15)

One is reminded of Sione de Beauvoir's observation on the young wife's position:

> To love her husband and to be happy is a duty she owes to herself and to society; it is what her family expects of her [...]. (481)

And

> [...] above all, a whole tradition enjoins upon wives the art of 'managing' a man; one must discover and humour his weaknesses and must cleverly apply in due measure flattery and scorn, docility and resistance, vigilance and leniency [...]. (487)

That Nanda Kaul refuses to buy this text, reflects her disapproval of the social ethos itself which percolates through this text.

Symbols: Mountain as 'Space': Ambiguity

From the very start the most noticeable aspect of the novel is its sense of geographical space. At the opening of the novel the author carefully and elaborately introduces the Kasauli and Carignano, the mountain and the house on its ridge.

At the beginning the mountain seems to be not only a real empirical space, but also a symbol of shelter, freedom, and fulfilment which Nanda Kaul at last receives after long years of unfulfilment; it is "the place [...] she had wanted and prepared for all her life" (3).

Paradoxically, even this space has not been free from violence as is shown by Ila Das's gruesome death.

The mountain has been made vivid and fascinating with its varied sights, its wide range of sounds, its smell, its occasional dust-storms, long spells of rain, sudden flowers bursting out after a night of rain. The reader can, as it were, share Nanda's peace, her cool solace, in this mountain reclusion. However, the mountain has not been envisioned here as an idyllic place. The threats of disharmony, cruelty, and violence are also there, and cannot be ignored. The author carefully weaves a network of details in order to bring out this duality.

Although the mountain is far away and high up from the mundane plains, yet painful memories of life in the big cities, remembrances of other locations where Nanda Kaul had suffered, where Tara is suffering right now, float back *en route* the protagonist's consciousness down memory lane.

At the end we also learn that coming to the mountain was not Nanda's own choice, that this was but the appropriate closure to her inwardly barren life, though after being compelled to settle down here all alone, she had persuaded to believe that she had at last found her real home and fulfilment.

As J. Jain observes:

> The world of Anita Desai's novels is an ambivalent one; it is a world where the central harmony is aspired to but not arrived at, and the desire to love and live clashes—at times violently—with the desire to withdraw and achieve harmony. Involvement and stillness are incompatible by their nature, yet they strive to exist together. (16)

Mountain: Geographic Location and Fictional Space

The geographical location of the mountain has been clearly indicated. At the same time it is also apparently a fictional space. This fictional space is marked by an essential ambiguity; this ambiguity, furthermore, corresponds to an ambiguity in Nanda's approach. Nanda seems to incarnate self-assurance; at the same time she is also haunted by innate uncertainties. She reflects both firmness and hesitation, both withdrawal from, and reaching out to, life. The mountain as fictional space does not scaffold a political/ social ideology; it rather relates to a feminine consciousness which is essentially ambiguous in its ambivalences between stark truth and the lure of fantasies.

Mountain: 'Heaven Haven'

When Nanda first came to the mountains it seemed to her like a "haven." As she tells Raka:

> When I first came here, I used to think of Gerard Manley Hopkins's poem [...]. I used to be reminded of it constantly:
>
> 'I have desired to go.
> Where springs not fail.
> To fields where flies no sharp and sided hail.
> And a few lilies blow.
> 'And I have asked to be.
> Where no storms come.
> Where the green swell is in the heavens dumb.
> And out of the swing of the sea.'
>
> 'Of course it was not written about a place, any place, but about a vocation—a nun's vocation, as it happens [...] but, all the same, it seemed to apply.'
>
> Her voice strengthened on this last line, grew brisk and lightened. (58)

It is significant that although Nanda is reminded of Hopkins's "Heaven-haven" she does not mythicise her "haven"; she knows it is "a place" (58). Indeed, the author gives no mythicised, or fantasized, or imaginary geography of the mountain as such. It is a real geography. Furthermore, the real geographical location is related to real historical facts of a colonial past. At the same time the place is made to imbibe imaginative meanings. The author makes it come alive by means of exquisite imaginative touches.

Mountain: Sweeping View

The mountain commands a sweeping view of the north and the south. But it is not a homogeneous view.

> In every direction there was a sweeping view—to the north, of the mountains, to the south, of the plains. Occasionally an eagle swam through this clear unobstructed mass of light and air. (4)

The north-facing windows of Nanda's house open "onto the blue waves of the Himalayas flowing out and up to the line of ice and snow sketched upon the sky" (4).

On the knoll of the house the wind is "keenest and the view widest" (4). On an afternoon, seen from the veranda,

> The hills were still sunlit, but the light was hazy, powdery. They seemed to be covered with a golden fuzz and melted into soft blues and violets in the distance. (27)

"Light and space" are "the two elements of the Kasauli view" (28).

> Here hills melted into the sky, sky into snows, snows into air. (28)

The hillsides look like water-colour paintings in mauve and violet (28).

After a rain one can get a glimpse of the extraordinary expanse of the scene.

> Away in the north the rock-scarred snow range glittered. To the south many hundreds of miles of the plain were visible, streaked with streams and pitted with bright pools of rain. (87)

Raka's resentment—at the suggestion of being sent to school— is blown away as she scrambles up to the top and sees before her "a breadth of space, a vast sweeping depth" (61). The scene spreads like an "an ancient scroll" unrolled:

> To the north, the soft, downy hills flowed, wave upon wave, gold and blue and violet and indigo, like the sea (61).

Dagshai and Sabathu look like "handful of pebbles gleaming on golden hilltops" (43). No wonder, Nanda remembers Hopkins's poem "Heaven-Haven" on her arrival at Kasauli.

Mountain: Blurring View: The Gorge and the Factory

The south-facing windows, however, on the other hand, "looked down the plunging cliff to the plains stretching out, flat and sere, to the blurred horizon" (4); "the cliff plunging seven thousand feet down to the Punjab plains" (13); "down the gorge with its gashes of red earth, its rocks and gullies and sharply spiked agaves, to the Punjab plains—a silver haze in the summer heat—stretching out to a dim yellow horizon." (17)

Thus the mountain seems to suggest an aspiration towards the infinite expanse and altitude of the serene blue peaks on the one hand, and a blurring, confused plunge into a dull vista of the shabby plains on the other. Is it symptomatic of Nanda's own predicament?

Again, for Raka the serene beauty of the scene from the hilltop is ecstasizing. Still the contrastive picture of the other end of the hill too obsesses her.

> [...] the lip of the cliff and the sudden drop down the red, rock-bespattered ravine to the plain that lay stretched out and heavy, the dusty pelt of a yellow animal panting in the sun. (41)

It is also hot in contrast to the cool north. The heat comes up from the plains to assault the cool of the mountain.

> The plain below opened wide its mouth and it was its oven breath that billowed up the mountainside [...]. (48)

The suggestion of an ugly animal writhing in heat is appropriately accompanied by the image of a demonic creature—"a square dragon" (42). It is the factory with its enormous concrete walls. To Raka the 'dragon' "seemed to dominate the landscape" (42). It is also the "central dagger" (48) piercing the sky, evoking the suggestion of violence and disharmony.

> The chimneys piercing the white sky, lashed about with black whips of smoke. (49)

Raka sniffs the air and smells cinder, serum, chloroform and spirit, things which are supposed to be anachronistic in an idyllic pastoral. It is the assault of the shabby seedy industrial scene upon the picturesque mountain resort.

> Sharp chimneys thrust out cushions and scarves of smoke *on the milky blue of the afternoon sky.* (emphasis added).

Perfectly in tune with this polluting presence are the

> chutes emerging from its back wall [...] built to disgorge factory waste into the ravine and immediately below them were small, squat structures that looked like brick kilns amongst the spiked, curved blades of the giant agaves that were, besides the pines, the only vegetation of that *blighted gorge.* (42; emphasis added)

In addition to this disturbing, 'blighting' presence on the mountain scape we are also reminded that "the army is everywhere" (57), and that "too many tourists" come up to scratch names and dates on trees, which stand out "as incongruous and obtrusive as the barbed wire" (57). A "frightening" instrument has also been set up on the hill which looks like an atomic reactor or "some such scientific monstrosity" (57). Nanda feels uneasy:

> Too many tourists. Too much army. How they are ruining this—this quiet place [...]. It really is—is saddening." (57)

You can recall Eliot's lines here:

> There is not even silence in the mountains [...]
>
> There is not even solitude in the mountains.

Carignano, on the hilltop may be safe, but the way downwards is hazardous for a lonely old woman (139). At the end Ila is killed by a black shape that detaches itself from "the last rock between her and the hamlet" (142), and springs soundlessly upon her like a preying beast. The mountain becomes the scene of predatory violence.

Mountain: Isolation

Isolation and remoteness add to the distinction of this mountain. It is not within easy reach of mundane life on the plains. One can trudge up to Carignano, Nanda's house on the top of one of the hills, only with difficulty. It also takes long to come up from the plains as it is far away from the big cities.

Mountain: Bare

The mountain is bare both literally and metaphorically. It is not the typical Indian hillscape which should normally contain one temple at least. Neither is there a fine, soothing, useful river which is common with Indian landscapes in literature. In its place we have only the ravine and the gorge receiving the factory waste.

No myths are attached to the place. Political waves or busy commerce do not reach this far-flung place. The only evidence of industrial operation is the medicine factory down the hills which is supposed to squeeze, crush and maul animals in order to make medicine,—serums for dog-bite.

Mountain: Barrenness

It is part of the Kasauli range of the Himalayas, the author points out, whose "chief virtue" is "barrenness" and "starkness" (4). It is this 'virtue' that appeals to Nanda.

> What pleased and satisfied her so, here at Carignano, was its barrenness. This was the chief virtue of all Kasauli of course—its starkness. It had rocks, it had pines. It had light and air. (4)

The author carefully brings out the austere aspect of the mountain. Nanda and Raka, the great-grandmother and great-granddaughter, walk together along:

> [...] the sere, silent hill-sides on which boulders seemed to have been arrested in downward motion and nothing grew on the pine-needle-spread earth but a few tangles of wild raspberries, hairy with thorn, and contorted agave. (57)

Carignano stands on a "bleached" ridge with its "orderly austerity." Raka likes this house. But she is more drawn by "the ravaged, destroyed and barren spaces of Kasauli [...] the ravine where yellow snakes slept under grey rocks and agaves growing out of the dust and rubble, the skeletal pines that rattled in the wind, the wind-levelled hilltops [...]" (91).

You can compare this description with some lines in Eliot's *The Waste Land;* for instance,

> What are the roots that clutch, what branches grow out of this stony rubbish?
>
> The dead tree gives no shelter, the cricket no relief [...]
>
> Dead mountain mouth of carious teeth that cannot spit [...].

Mountain: Flora: Austere

The vegetation life in the mountain is in tune with this barrenness. Pine and cicada,—again like *The Waste Land*—are the plants of this rock, and Nanda finds them appropriate and acceptable. Throughout the novel one is reminded of the presence of the pine and cicada trees. They are present visibly and audibly. In the very opening sentence of the novel we have them. Before seeing the postman Nanda Kaul pauses "under the pine trees to take in their scented sibilance and listen to the cicadas fiddling invisibly under the mesh of pine needles." Nanda wants no postman, no interference from the world below. Among the pines and cicadas she seeks her refuge, solace, companion.

She asked to be left to the pines and cicadas alone.

At the approach of the postman Nanda steps "backward into the garden and the wind suddenly billowed up and threw the pine branches about as though to curtain her" (3). At this point Nanda's likeness with the pine trees is obvious,—the author indeed highlights this—and she feels a strong desire to be merged into one.

> She was grey, tall and thin and her silk sari made a sweeping, shivering sound and she fancied she could merge with the pine trees and be mistaken for one. To be a tree, no more and no less, was all she was prepared to undertake. (4)

The pine trees under which Nanda stands, characteristically "stood by the gate in their exaggerated attitudes as of men going up in flames with their arms outstretched, charred, too, about the trunks [...]."

The pines have their own beauty for Nanda to perceive. Waiting for Raka to arrive, Nanda sees that "on the knoll and the gate the wind ruffled the pine needles so that they glistened silver in the sunlight" (36).

Besides the pine and cicada there are the "thorny snatchful(s) of raspberries" (5), which the truant schoolboy looks for. The clumps of Iris at Carignano had "finished blooming" (4).

Mountain: Flora: Greenery

However, in spite of the pervasive barrenness the stark, bare hills have their rare patches of colour as well. It may be noted that at least the chestnut tree at the foot of the hill is "leafy" (4). The pastor,—one of the previous owners of Carignano—had

> [...] found it sad that its exposed situation on the ridge made it impossible to plant the cottage garden he would have liked but he did plant three apricot trees where the house sheltered them from the worst gales, and they flourished in the stony soil and bore fruit.

Now the north wall of Nanda's house is "washed by the blue shadows of the low, dense apricot trees" (5).

In the deserted burnt house on the hills there are only dry pebbles. But Nanda knows better and tells Raka:

> It looks dreadful [...] but one shower of rain will bring out hundreds of flowers—lilies, dahlias that the old woman had planted. (57)

And in the morning after the first rain Raka wakes up to find "hosts of wild zephyranthes that had come up in the night" (88). Damp lilies have also come out, though damp lilies in the milk jug on the table rather remind Raka of her mother, ill in a nursing home, under a pink blanket (89).

The bloom is, however, too brief; dust and aridity are the norm:

> The pink lilies folded up and disappeared. The plains were swallowed up by the yellow dust again. The sun frizzled the grasses and blazed on the rocks of Kasauli. All was either bleached or blackened by heat and glare. (92)

Mountain: Fauna: Idyllic Pastoral

As the pine is the chief plant of this mountain, the eagle is the fauna of this space. Carignano has a sweeping view in every direction with an occasional eagle swimming through the clear unobstructed mass of light and air.

As Nanda waits for Raka's arrival—rather annoyed—an eagle sweeps into ken a thousand feet below,

> [...] its wings outspread, gliding on currents of air without once moving its great muscular wings which remained in repose, in control. She had wished, it occurred to her, to imitate that eagle-gliding with eyes closed. (19)

Raka too has similar feelings while looking at the eagles. Reaching the Monkey Point Raka has the ecstatic feeling that she would fly like an eagle:

> [...] if she let go [...] she would fly, fly off the hilltop and down, down on currents of air, like the eagles that circled slowly, regally below her. (61)

The pastor, the second owner of Carignano, delighted at his success with the apricot trees, had

> bought a marble bird bath at a sale held at the Garden House whose owners, the aged sisters Abbott, died within a week of each other and whose goods were auctioned off, and placed it under the trees. It was his joy to watch the bulbuls and hoopoes come to feast on the apricots and flutter down into the bird bath and plunge and preen and scatter the water in spray. (6-7)

There are a few fine strokes suggesting an idyllic pastoral peace and beauty. As Nanda, rather annoyed at receiving a letter, looks intently at the vast uninterrupted expanse, "a large white and yellow butterfly crossed over, disturbing her concentration" (13). On another occasion Nanda is seen leaning on the gate of Carignano, her eyes resting on the mauve and violet hillsides, when "cattle browsed homewards to small hidden hamlets in the valleys," and "all grey softer and grayer" (28), as if in tune with her own graceful ageing. When Raka scrambles up the Monkey Point, and Nanda is left sitting below,

> unseeing, she almost ran into a goat, then a kid, then a whole herd that came springing down, leapt over her back and flew like birds, landing at Nanda Kaul's feet and tripping nimbly homewards, the small goatherd casually whistling and sauntering after them. (60)

Once the author envisions the mountain as a flock of sheep. The "woolen hills" (65) is a fine expression evoking the scanty grassy coat over the rocks as well as the coat of a sheep. The pastoral connotations of sheep and shepherd hardly need to be stressed.

Mountain: Fauna: Predatory

There are varieties of birds, animals, reptiles, insects on the mountain. It seems to be less a world of humans than of other creatures; whereas some of these creatures seem to hail from a pastoral idyll, many other references to these creatures of the mountain often carry disturbing suggestions of ferocity, cruelty, violence, or rot.

Thus vultures are a common feature of this mountain-scape. It is perhaps natural that the high-soaring bird fascinates the freedom-loving souls. But it may also be noted that the eagle is a predatory bird as well; its circling, soaring and gliding are punctuated by its search for prey. Similarly the vulture's circling indicates dead flesh and rot. Raka, on her lonely prowling on the hills, sees "in the sky, huge vultures circling lazily, stealthily, on currents of air, prowling for game" (43). Once the child is scared. As she slides down as usual on her way towards the direction of the factory, suddenly there is a vulture:

> A vulture had moved its claws up a little, shrugged its massive shoulders, stretched out its rubber-hose neck and belched. The child started. Then walked backwards, away from the tree. Turning around abruptly, she dropped on all fours and scrambled up the hill so fast [...]. (73)

It does not seem to be a very safe world for the child; though she moves about unharmed, there are potential threats all the time. Once on her lonely exploration of the hill Raka comes upon "a great, thick, yellow snake poured in rings upon itself, basking on the sunned top of a flat rock"; this is her first view of "a loose soft sackful of snakes" (49). Even before this she has glimpses of "the tips of snakes' tails parting the cracks of rocks" and "slit eyes watching" her from the shade, and has heard the "slither of scales" upon the ground (49).

Besides this there are also the "wild horde" of black-faced *langurs* who are not meek at all; they are mentioned as "those fierce, lithe panthers of the monkey world, more feline than simian" (58). There are the jackals and dogs. Ram Lal confidentially tells Raka about "the ghosts of people who have died of dog-bite and snake-bite" and "roam on the hillsides" (44). The old man warns the child about the ravine: "See those chutes? They empty the bones and ashes of dead animals down into the ravine" (44). These are animals supposedly used in the factory and subsequently thrown away as waste, a principal attraction for the vultures which circle above the ravine. Ram Lal cautions Raka:

> Jackals come at night to chew the bones. Then they go mad and bite the village dogs. The mad dogs run around, biting people [...]. It isn't safe, hear? (44)

Even smaller creatures seem to be part of the pervasive predatory pattern. As Nanda, strolling in her garden, flings away a squashed apricot,

> Immediately, a bright hoopoe, seeing its flight and flash, struck down at it and tore at its bright flesh, then flew off with a lump in its beak. It had its nest in the eaves outside her bedroom window [...]. Their [the nestlings'] screams were shrill and could madden. (4)

Sitting under the shade of her veranda Nanda watches a pair of bulbuls quarrelling, falling in a flurry of feathers to the ground; they

> [...] stirred up a small frenzy of dust, then shot off in opposite directions, scolding and abusing till a twist of a worm distracted them. (13)

Such passages automatically remind one of Ted Hughes's bird poems. For example, one can cite Hughes's "Thrushes":

> Terrifying are the attent sleek thrushes on the lawn More coiled steel than living—a poised Dark deadly eye, those delicate legs
>
> Triggered to stirrings beyond sense—with a start, a bounce, a stab

Overtake the instant and drag out some writhing thing.

It is a similar de-romanticised and intent view of the world of birds and beasts. When apricots run out the hoopoe has to make up "by catching moths in mid-air and dragging worms out of the earth" (65). While attending to Ila's telephone call Nanda watches "the white hen drag out a worm inch by resisting inch from the ground till it snapped in two [...]. She winced at its mutilation" (21); but the hen continues "greedily gulping down bits of worm" (22). Of course this is a compulsion on the part of the poor bird. And a similar compulsion goads the herd of goats in the deserted ravine, "nibbling at the sparse thorns and nettles with rubber-lipped greed and nervous avarice" (73). Surely not an idyllic picture of a pastoral!

Even withindoors, inside her own room Raka "met a spider that groomed its hairs in a corner, saw lizard's eyes blinking out of a dark groove" (41).

> The cuckoos are the only birds in the abandoned unfinished building on the knoll. They sang and sang invisibly. These were not the dutiful domestic birds that called Nanda Kaul to attention at Carignano. They were the demented birds that raved and beckoned Raka on to a land where there was no sound, only silence, no light, only shade, and skeletons kept in beds of ash on which the footprints of jackals flowered in grey" (90).

Mountain: Sound: Harmonious

Like a living being the mountain has its own smells and sounds which have been clearly and elaborately mentioned. Some sounds originate from the fauna, some from the trees, some in the wind, so much so that humans appear redundant in the scheme. The very opening sentence evokes the "sibilance" of the pines and the "fiddling" of cicadas,

> Nanda Kaul paused under the pine trees to take in their scented sibilance and listen to the cicadas fiddling invisibly under the mesh of fine needles. (3)

This seems to be the appropriate music of the place, and not the club music which seems incongruous and vulgar on the hills. For the lonely old woman in the old empty house

> There were only the cicadas to be heard, a sound so even and so insubstantial that it seemed to emerge from the earth itself [...] a scent of pine-needles made audible. (13)

As Raka stealthily enters the empty clubhouse during one hot summer afternoon, it was as if "all Kasauli slept except for the cicadas that sawed and fiddled without stop" (43).

At the beginning we are told that all Nanda wants at this fag end of her life is "the sound of the cicadas and the pines" (19). The other sound acceptable to her is the music of the withered rose-creeper in Carignano, which is "an exhausted mass of grey creaks and groans" (17). Towards the end when Nanda and Ila, the two old ladies talk in the empty garden cicadas "audibly sizzled" under the sun (103). Raka wanders about in the mountain "in a kind of dream, set to the sound of cicadas and the wind in the pines" (64). Nanda and Raka stand gazing at the withering flowers; under these "a cicada shrilled and whirred frenziedly" (73). As R. Kundu writes in "The Female Quest for Identity [...]" *(Feminist English Literature,* ed. Bhatnagar; New Delhi, 1999): "The narration, remarkable for its swift pace as well as care for small details, acquires its special mood by means of the never-ceasing dirge of pines and cicadas that presides over the story" (119).

The pine and the cicada, and the keen wind together produce the music of the mountain. These are the mountain's own sound, and part of its aloof, rugged grandeur. Just as the hills look like sea waves from the top, the sound of the wind too, "rushing up through the pines and then receding was the *sound of the sea"* (61).

There are also a few instances of soft sounds. For example, as Nanda weaves her stories to Raka the rooks "cawed," and afterwards the "owls began to call softly, experimentally" (99). Again, on the eve of the arrival of Raka Nanda feels annoyed, and remembers her earlier desire to be only like the high- soaring eagle.

> Then a cuckoo called, quite close, here in her garden, very sofdy, very musically, but definitely calling—she recognized its domestic voice. (19)

Mountain: Sound: Disharmony

Alongside the superb music mentioned above we are also invited to listen to another range of notations which are not so grand or harmonious, but can be rather disturbing. For example, the terror of the dust-storm is captured in a powerful auditory image; Raka sees a storm-tossed bird:

> A white hen was lifted into the air and tossed past the window in a frantic, fluttery arc, its squawks snatched out of its beak and shattered like glass. (53)

Jackals howl at night; Raka, in her hiding place behind the club hall where revelry is going on, is scared by the howling. Ahead of her, no longer on the ground but at some distance now, her mother crying. Then it was a jackal crying (72)

As Raka scrambles uphill, she starts

> small avalanches of pebble and loud, clanking ones of empty tins. She disturbed the crickets and made them raise their voices in alarm [...]. It was complicated, shrill incessant and Raka shook and shook her head to get the buzz out. (49-50)

As Nanda Kaul and Raka walk homewards in the gathering darkness, the "great silence" is "rent now and then by the clear, ringing call of some invisible bird that defied night" (62). The sounds Raka imagines amidst an "eerie" soundlessness are disturbing. As the child looks at the distant forest fire from her window,

> Holding her ear to the cold pane closely, she thought she heard the cries of animals and birds burning in that fire. But when she removed her ear from the pane she heard only the crepitation of silence. Once, the soft hooting of an owl. (75)

The soft hooting of the night-bird mingles into the eerie silence of the night instead of dispelling it.

Again, when the rain comes it is like a kind of climax after the high wind "whining" through the pine trees all afternoon and the clouds gathering like "a great polar bear crouching" and "what rain! The house shook, the roof crackled, long raindrops slanted in" (81). As the rain continues outside, Nanda spins her stories for Raka, "raising her voice above the drumming of the rain on the roof and the booming and echoing of thunder in the hills that followed the rain like hunting horns" (86).

Mountain as Literary Space

In the tradition of pagan, European and oriented concepts the mountain has stood for an idealized position since ages.

The Greeks placed the abode of their gods on the Olympian mount. The Christians too would opt for the myth of sermons 'on the Mount.' The high profile gods of the Hindu pantheon are supposed to haunt the Indian mountains.

To the traditional Indian imagination the mountain has been a spiritual place/space. The Himalaya is called *Devaatmd.* It is also the recluse of monks and ascetics who give up the material world, and the route to *mahaprasthanam* or the grand exit, supposedly leading to heaven.

To the European/English romantic imagination mountain was a common image for the detachment/aloofness/sweeping view of the poet. After the war people sought the mountains as shelter or sanatoria for the 'magic' (*The Magic Mountain* of Thomas Mann) of healing.

In the British colonial writings about India in particular, references to Indian mountains frequently measured them against English landscape which was taken as the norm. To the colonial imagination Indian mountains offered an image of threat as well as lure, and thus became synonym for mystery. The lure and threat that epitomized India as the 'Other,' seemed to acquire intensified manifestation in its hills and mountains. Forster's Marabar Hills (in *A Passage to India),* for example, represents the region of 'mystery'/'muddle,' offering neither solace, nor peace, nor detachment. Kipling articulates a similar sense of awe at the reductive mystery of the great grey hills which made one feel dwarfed and insignificant (*The Heart of a Maid,* 1890).

In *Journey to Ithaca,* a later novel of Anita, people, including two Italians, end up at the higher regions of the Himalayas in course of their search for peace and spiritual fulfilment. But *Fire on the Mountain* introduces an unusual mountain space with no myth or conventional adages attached to it. It is a very real place of the free wind booming through the hills, of dust storm that rage and tear the rocks, of rain and thunder, of prolonged aridity and devastating forest-fires, of snow-white peaks and red-yellow gorge blighted by factory-waste, of high-soaring eagles and carrion-seeking vultures. Still Anita projects it in such a way that the mountain itself becomes a trope. In Anita Desai's hands it is neither mystery, nor divine, but still it is a trope as it becomes the 'space' for a woman.

Though in the early years of her settling at Kasauli Nanda Kaul is reminded of Hopkins's "Heaven-haven," she does not mythicise her "haven"; she knows it is "a place" (58) after all. Similarly, the author too gives no mythicised, or fantasized or imaginary geography as such. Rather she shows a sense of historicity by relating the geographical location of her novel to the colonial past of India. At the same time, however, real geography has been made to imbibe imaginative meanings as it is made to come alive by means of exquisite imaginative touches.

Thus the mountain in *Fire on the Mountain* emerges to be a parallel to Nanda in her isolation and withering, as well as in her elegance, grandeur. The fictionalized mountain space emerges as a site that symbolically implies Nanda Kaul's tragic predicament as well as her wistful dream,—the long- cherished and long-suppressed longing for 'a room of her own,' a world of her own.

Mary Daly observes at the beginning of her book, *Gynt Ecology* (1987): "Patriarchy appears to be everywhere. Even outer space and the future have been colonized." Women writers across the world today have been constructing worlds of isolation as a way of escaping and de-recognizing this patriarchal domination. Canadian writer Aritha Van Herk's *Places far from Ellesmere* (1990) is a typical example; here the author envisions an escape into a far-flung Canadian island in the twentieth century along with a nineteenth century heroine, Tolstoy's Anna Karenina. She assures Anna that here in this island Anna will be at least saved from the harsh old man *(i.e.* Tolstoy), and will be allowed to survive instead of being forced to end herself on the rails. Aritha Van Herk constructs an imaginative geography. Ellesmere is an imaginary geographical location which stands for a mental space for women like Anna who had been, according to Van Herk, mauled by an unfeeling society which was insensitised by patriarchal ideology through centuries. Ellesmere promises Anna a "writing place: hiding place," which is free from patriarchal domination. Whereas Tolstoy is bent on killing Anna, Van Herk assures her survival by smuggling her into this space where, in spite of the harsh weather and other material discomforts, Anna would get the space to pause, to sit down and think freely.

As an island Ellesmere becomes emblematic of the woman's vision of a woman's utopia; it is free from all inhibiting constructs of the big cities, as also their shabbiness, seediness, squalor, filth. It is covered with white snow, harsh but pure. Arriving at Ellesmere itself becomes a symptomatic act of celebration of 'her' selfhood, a kind of fulfilment. The author extends her invitation not only to Anna but to all the Active characters who have suffered at the hand of their male authors and would have longed to be free from the oppressive voyeurism and assault of their respective authors and readers.

> You are at Ellesmere. You have escaped to Ellesmere. 'Her' island, *tabula rasa,* a wayness so thoroughly truant you have cut all connexion to all places far from Ellesmere. This is what you long for. Anna must have too. (77)

But whereas Van Herk's Ellesmere, a fictive space, and isolated arctic island, epitomizes unambiguous self-assurance and assertion of the woman, the mountain of Desai seems to offer a different and ambiguous signal. Perhaps this ambiguity is necessarily embedded in the very nature of the space she has chosen. An island can be isolated and autonomous. In another novel of Anita Desai, *Where Shall I Go This Summer?,* the protagonist (Sita) longs for an island in order to overcome a personal crisis. She would assert:

> What I'm doing is trying to escape from the madness here, escape to a place where it might be possible to be sane again. (1982: 35)

But a mountain is not autonomous in that sense. The distant snowy peaks are the inaccessible utopia. But at the other end the mountain slopes down into mundane hamlets where brutal death soundlessly springs upon Ila Das from behind the dark rock. So it does not necessarily follow that the self-actualising journey of a woman can achieve its goal in the mountains. Nevertheless, it is the end of the road for Nanda Kaul, "privacy achieved only at the very end of her life" (36), and the "best" home (91) for Raka who had always seemed to lack the ticket to social life.

The basic paradox highlighted by the geography of the story is that one cannot occupy a bounded or enclosed cultural space, howsoever one may long for the same. It is true that the human society, however little of it is there on the hills, remains largely invisible. It is also true that the human world of the plains seems remote from Carignano or the other hilltops like Aritha Van Herk's 'Ellesmere' island (seen from Herk's island), "the world exists in some enigmatic novel far beyond" (121). Still the fact remains that it is an eroded hill that has received the beatings of the weather; the purity of the hill is threatened by the factory; its smoke lashes the white sky; its smell of chemicals fills the air. It is haunted by violence. Even Carignano, Nanda's 'glass palace' *(a la* Amitav Ghosh) on the high ridge, is invaded by the outer world, as has been suggested by the postman at the beginning and by the telephone towards the end of the story.

Otima, the unhappy wife and mother of unhappy children in Desai's *Voices in the City,* also withdrew into the mountains of Kalimpong, her favourite hill station, but this is a decision she comes to regret later. As she writes to her daughter Amla,

> I reproach myself for having come to Kalimpong [...] I should have kept on your father's house in Calcutta, made house for you children there [...]. I had always dreamt of Kalimpong, Amla, even in the best of years. Now I know I made the decisions and changes too abruptly, without thinking clearly [...]. It is my fault [...]. And the day was lovely. I could see the villages in the valley below [...]. The Kanchenajunga hidden by the whitest fleece of clouds. All the woods blue and misty. And my garden lifting out of the rainwater, so brilliant. But it seems my instincts have all been wrong, my paradise a fool's abode, and I have lost touch with my closest ones [...]. (1982: 201-02)

Fire on the Mountain may be categorized as 'geografictione,' to use the term coined by Aritha Van Herk to denote a species of narration which combines geography with fiction, and creates its own geography as it cuts out its own specific narrative space. *Fire on the Mountain* represents this trend in fiction, which, instead of using place as backdrop, reinterprets it and rein scribes it with fresh meaning.

Desai's treatment of the mountain as space is an emblem of her *ecriture feminine* and thus offers the possibility of fresh, varied, contrary and multiple interpretations.

For the perceptive reader, the configuration and etching of Kasauli in Desai's novel are resonant with intertextual echoes from various sources, and especially from *The Waste Land;* the pine and cicada, the crickets, the ruined house (even to the cawing bird on its roof), the barren rocks, the wrecked solitude ("There is not even silence in the mountains/There is not even solitude in the mountains") are some of the unmistakable traces left by

Eliot's poem. But it seems significant that whereas Eliot's waste land was blessed at the end by thunder and rain, here the story finally comes to a halt at a richly ambiguous open ending, with the strong forest fire quickly spreading across the mountains.

Symbol of Fire

There have been recurrent references to forest-fires on the mountain. These can burst anywhere unpredictably, and bring devastation in its train. Such fires leave scars which remain visible long afterwards, and see beyond healing. The novel ends with a fire. And from the beginning through carefully accumulated suggestions the reader is prepared for the final fire.

At the start it is a series of references to, or reports of, previous fires. Then there is an actual fire, though still seen from a distance. At the end Raka herself sets the forest on fire. Early in the novel we have a proleptic hint. The pine trees under which Nanda stands, characteristically "stood by the gate in their exaggerated attitudes as of men going up in flames with their arms outstretched, charred, too, about the trunks [...]" (12). Nanda wishes to be one such tree: "She would be a charred tree-trunk in the forest" (23).

During the dust storm Ram Lal is worried, because "this is how forest fires do start. I can't tell you how many forest fire we see each year in Kasauli" (53); the many burnt trees and houses around the hills bear evidence to Ram Lal's report. Ram Lal tells Raka the story of the burnt house on one of the hilltops, where the resident, "an English Mem" had gone mad after failing to rescue her cat from the fire. A proleptic touch is added to the story as Nanda Kaul relates it to Raka:

> Up on the hill there, Raka, you will see the burnt black shell of a house. It was burnt down in a terrible forest fire [...]. An old lady lived there alone and they say she went mad and was put away. Poor woman, I wonder if she would not have preferred to die in the fire. (57)

Raka feels a strange attraction towards the images and relics of fire. She stealthily visits the burnt house, and imagines herself a tree in flames.

The first time Raka sees a forest fire far away, "it was like a fire in a dream—silent, swift and threatening [...] spilling down the hillside in runnels of sparks, in streams of heat" (74).

The novel closes with the sound, flame and smoke of a spreading fire.

One can also compare this with the prairie novels of Canada, in which fire is frequently used as an unpredictable and uncontrollable natural calamity—often with symbolic overtones.

Critical Responses

In his article, "Images of Alienation—a Study of Anita Desai's Novels," S.P. Swain writes:

> In Anita Desai's novels, imagery lends a poetic, lyrical colouring to the problems of the estranged self and project reality through "artistic parallels more powerful and eloquent than common collocation of words" (Prasad 1984: 54). Besides enriching the artistic and aesthetic value of the novels, images in Desai, enlarge the critical and interpretative horizon of her art. They suggest the protagonist's totality of experience and build up the overall tonality of the novels. Images in Desai are not confined to the world of art only. There are scientific images too. Both these images produce esthetic effects and impart a tangible shape to stirred up emotional states of the alienated self. To Anita Desai, "it is the image that matters, the symbol, the myth" (Srivastava 1984: 04). There is in her a persistent search for the most appropriate symbols and images in the expression of the subterranean and the subconscious [...].

In *Fire on the Mountain,* Nanda Kaul wants to withdraw from the milieu and merge with the pine trees. Free from all "unwelcome intrusion and distraction" (3), she longs for the privacy, seclusion, tranquility and solidity of trees: "She stepped, backwards into the garden and the wind suddenly billowed up and threw the pine branches about as though to curtain her" (3). The news of Raka's visit to Carignano shatters Nanda's hope for privacy and isolation. Raka's arrival would pose a threat to her "privacy achieved only at the very end of her life" (36). The image of the "yellow rose-creeper" that "had blossomed so youthfully last month but was now reduced to an exhausted mass of grey creaks and groans again" (17), symbolises the wilting and withering of her hope for a cloistered life [...].

Raka's isolation is instinctive and unimposed. It is spontaneous and natural. It is the isolation of a roe, playful and fanciful. She could often be found: "[...] scrambling up a stony hillside [...] or wandering down a lane in a slow straying manner, stopping to strip a thorny bush of its few berries or to examine an insect under a leaf [...]" (46).

Wishing to be left to the pines and cicadas, Nanda withdraws herself totally from the world of "bags and letters, messages and demands, requests, promises and queries" (3). Raka and Nanda, components of "the bareness and stillness of the Carignano garden," of "the starkness of rocks, pines and mountains" (4), want no one and nothing else. Seeking an absolute isolation here, she fancies she could merge with the pine trees and be mistaken for one. "To be a tree, no more and no less" (4) is all she desires. She wants to be alone and to have Carignano to herself in this period of her life, "when stillness and calm were all that she wished to entertain" (17). The imagery used highlights Nanda Kaul's longing for a secluded and still life. Nanda despises almost everyone who comes her way: her haughty, complacent daughter, Asha, her pale and fragile granddaughter Tata, her elusive, volatile and cadaverous great-granddaughter Raka and her old, decrepit and emaciated companion Ila Das [...].

In *Fire on the Mountain,* Raka is "a mosquito flown up from the plains to tease and worry" (40). Raka (literally means the moon) is ironically likened to one of "those dark crickets that leap in fright but do not sing" (39). She is "lizard-like" (42), "a pet insect" (54), "higher than the eagles" (61), or "a mosquito, minute and fine" (39). Raka moves about in Kasauli like a 'soundless moth,' solitary and isolated. Nanda Kaul views Raka as "an uninvited mouse or cricket" (85), stealthily entering the barren and rugged world of Carignano. Pining for a secluded life, she would lie down motionless like "a lizard on a stone wall" (23).

Through zoological images, Anita Desai juxtaposes the animal world with the human to suggest the cannibalistic and predatory nature of man. Preet Singh's sexual assault on Ila Das, for instance. Ila's cold-blooded rape and murder is gruesome and horrifying. Carnal images indicate our low instincts and desires, our base and ignoble motives. Reference to animals serves as an interface imagery.

The house in *Fire on the Mountain* is a static and iterative image appearing in clusters with the image of the garden and other botanical and inorganic images as portrayed in the picture of the Carignano: the house that consoles Nanda and satisfies her:

> She turned around and gazed at her house instead, simple and white and shining on the bleached ridge. On the north side, the wall was washed by the blue shadows of the low, dense apricot trees. On the east wall the sun glared, scoured and sharp. It seemed so exactly right as a house for her, it satisfied her heart completely. (5)

Nanda Kaul's house becomes her refuge. Desai sharply contrasts this with "that house—his house, never hers," (18) the perfect house she dutifully ran for her husband and family but to which she never really belonged.

Carignano, the desolate and haunted house in Kasauli inscapes the life of Nanda. But unlike Sita, she does not live in Carignano by choice. She lives there under compulsion deserted by her sons and daughters after the death of her husband. Yet she is content with its stark, secluded end sunny splendour. Symbolically, the seclusion and serenity of Carignano defines the stillness and freedom, Nanda has been able to achieve in her old age. Carignano is Nanda and Nanda Carignano. The humming and hectic part of Carignano is made out of Nanda's own past—the past that goes back to her days as a house-wife. It is juxtaposed with her awfully busy life in the past—ordering "too many servants" (29) entertaining "too many guests" (29) and tending "so many children" (29) and grandchildren. But Carignano, like Nanda, is buried in the silent spaces of inner vastness.

The image of the burnt house "at the top of the hill" (90) used in Chapter 18, Part-II, of the novel, mirrors the wild and unbridled nature of Raka with her irrepressible desire to set the forest on fire and her irresistible attraction towards "the ravaged, destroyed and barren spaces in Kasauli" (91).

At the top of the hill was the burnt house she had come to visit. It was only the charred shell of a small stone cottage. The verandah roof was already torn off and flung onto the hillside, the paving stones on the floor were cracked and gaping. The doors swung rotten, the window-frames hung askew, shattered glass lay amongst the cinders. The stairs were a tumable of rocks and weeds [...] (90).

The house imagery used in this novel is chiefly functional in nature. The house in this novel has its own history, that relentlessly links Nanda to other tormented and exiled women. Even this tranquil mountain resort, Carignano, that resonates in Nanda's experience, explodes and culminates in the rape and murder of her childhood friend, and alter ego, Ila Das [...].

The simple but dramatically powerful images in Desai trace the growth of the self from a state of seething discontent and despair to a state of psychic submission and spiritual consolation. Images of anguish in the external world of sights and sounds mature to images of spiritual identification of the inner world of the psyche. Rhythmically condensed, subtly chiselled colour images are neatly woven into the characters to point out the emotional chiaroscuro through successive stages of alienation leading to self-identification" *(IWE* 5).

About Anita Desai's use of symbols Sandhyarani Das writes in her article "The Ironic Presence of Nature in the Novels of Anita Desai" (Chapter 17 of her book, *The Novels of Anita Desai: A Critical Study):*

> The barren rocks and hills of Carignano becomes the projection of Nanda Kaul's self. She is herself lonely, has kept herself aloof from relatives and the society to spend a life of seclusion in the quiet house at Kasauli. The barren landscape, the lonely pine tree, the rocks and hills of Carignano do not provide her the absolute tranquility of her dreams. It is Raka's intrusion on the one hand and the consciousness of the grim realities of life on the other come on her way.

The screams of the hoopoes are shrill and maddening. Nanda Kaul rushes to pick up a bright apricot which falls down from the tree and is squashed by its fall. Suddenly she finds a bright hoopoe coming down and tearing at its bright flesh and flying off with a lump in its beak. The sight "did not fill her with delight" *(Fire on the Mountain* 4).

The house at Carignano has a history of violence, murder and death. Nanda Kaul had come here with the desire to enjoy the "stillness and calm" but the letter from her daughter Asha perturbs. She leans over the wooden railing at the back of the house where the yellow rose creeper had blossomed "so youthfully" last month but now reduced to an "exhausted mass of grey creaks and groans" again. Her desire for privacy and freedom, which she could never get as the Vice-Chancellor's wife and for which she has come to the hillside is suggested through the image of the eagle:

> An eagle swept over it, far below her, a thousand feet below, its wings out-spread, gliding on currents of air without once moving its great muscular wings which remained in repose, in control. She had wished, it occurred to her, to imitate that eagle gliding, with eyes closed. (19)

She watches a lapwing in the mustard fields beyond the garden hedge, "its uneven flapping flight through the funeral moon light." The cries of the nervous bird sharpens her sense of loneliness:

> Herself a grey cat, a night prowler, she watched it till it disappeared in that direction of the river, its cries growing fainter. Then rubbing her foot in the grass, she relished the sensation of being alone again. (26)

The garden in the Vice-Chancellor's quarters that was full of trees. Full of too many marauding parrots and squirrels and also too many children who "raided them for fruit" is an extended metaphor of the busy and hectic life of Nanda Kaul among children, relatives and guests. In contrast, the garden of Carignano is an image of bareness and emptiness. She does not want any addition to the garden, which like herself has arrived at a state of "elegant perfection," through a process of age, withering away and elimination. She also does not want to add anything to her own "pared, reduced and radiantly single life." Mien Raka comes she explores the hills and rocks of Kasauli and gets merged with them for hours together. Like Nanda, Raka wants only one thing; "to be left alone and pursue her own secret life amongst the rocks and pines of Kasauli" (48). She has all the "jealous, guarded instinct" of an explorer.

The destructive aspect of Nature is suggested by images of violence and destruction. The Pasteur Institute is an image of violence where the doctors make serum for injections for dog bites. They kill the mad dogs and use them for tests. They throw the bones and ashes of dead animals into the ravine and jackals come at night to that place to chew the bones. The "forest fire" is a threat to the quiet and undisturbed lives of the people of the hillside. Nanda Kaul tells Raka that a whole village may burn in a fire that big. Raka hears the cries of animals and birds burning that fire. The next morning she finds "a cindery smell" and a layer of ashes that is deposited on Kasauli like a "grey pelt."

The group of langurs with their destructive habits attract Raka. She runs towards them with Ram Lal yelling and waving her arms as they tear leaves off the apricot trees in search of fruit, pluck the flowers and destroy them, dash into the kitchen and grab at potatoes, "baring their teeth and gibbering at whoever came in the way." The sight of destruction fascinates her. The single house on the hills and another unbuilt one attract her like a "strong sea current." There is something "illegitimate, uncompromising and lawless—that made her tingle. The scene of devastation and failure somehow drew her, inspired her" (90).

Through the image of prey and predator Desai depicts the violence in Nature. The hoopoe catching the 'moths' in the mid-air and 'ragging worms out of earth and fighting with the bulbuls are a few instances of such images:

> [...] Closer to closer, the hoopoe promenaded under the apricot trees, smartly and unfurling the striped fan on top of its head. Its young had flown and it appeared to be celebrating, even flaunting its independence, its new youth and freedom. It pounced upon a grasshopper and stabbed it to death with its victorious beak (103-04).

When Ila Das telephones Nanda and informs her of her arrival in Carignano, Nanda Kaul becomes distracted for some time. She babbles on the telephone and Nanda turns her head the other way in an effort to escape but she finds a white hen dragging out a worm "inch by resisting inch" from the ground till it "snapped in two." Nanda feels herself like the worm. The violence in the animal world is slowly transferred to the human world. The boys tease Ila Das like langurs. They swing about her long arm and hoot at her little grey top knot and wobble on top of her head, "whooping and hooting, munching and mooing, they ran to the right and left of her, suddenly swerving to bump into her small, brittle person, to send her crocheted and moth eaten shoulders bag flying or her umbrella spinning [...]" (108).

These acts of violence at last culminate in the rape and tragic death of Ila Das by Preet Singh and his gang. In the evening when Ila Das comes through the forest path Preet Singh behaves roughly with her. The figure of Preet Singh emerging from the rocks is a ghastly sight in the still quiet hillside:

> Just then a black shape detached itself from the jagged pile of the rock, that last rock between her and the hamlet, and sprang soundlessly at her. She staggered under its weight with a gasp that ripped through her chest. It had her by the throat. She struggled, choking Dying to stretch and stretch and stretch that gasp till it becomes a shout, a shout that the villagers would hear, the red dog would hear, a shout for help. (142)

But nobody comes to her help. The fingers of Preet Singh tighten and Ila Das lies dead; "crushed back, crushed down into the earth, she lay raped, broken, still and finished (143).

The news of the tragic death of Ila Das shatters Nanda Kaul's world of reverie into pieces. The illusory world which she had created as on emotional shelter completely breaks down: She had dropped the telephone. With her head still thrown back, for back, she gasped: No, no it is all lie! No, it cannot be. It was a lie—Ila was not trapped, not dead. She had lied to Raka, lied about everything (145).

She realises that all the "graces and glories" with which she has tried to captivate Raka are only a fabrication, tranquillizer pills, which helped her to sleep at night. Nanda Kaul's attempt to escape reality like Sita's escape to Manori in *Where Shall We Go This Summer* is an exercise in self-deception. Complete involvement in 'undiluted illusion represented by Ila Das or "undiluted illusion" like that of Nanda Raul, both eventually spell tragedy (Prasad M., *Anita Desai: The Novelist* 102).

The fire that Raka sets to the forest is expressive of her resolve to destroy Nanda Raul's world of make-believe. It is not merely an act of violence as Francine E. Krishna says, but also "an act of Purification as if she might burn away the lies and deceit of Nanda's portrayal of her childhood as well as the violence of her own" (Rrishna F., *Indian Literature* 169).

There is always an interaction between the human and the non-human world as much of the imagery this novel deal with the animate non-human features of Nature and the landscape like animals, birds and insects. These images are not static rather they change according to the change within the characters. For example when Raka is strolling with Nanda Raul and happens to see the langur they seem to her funny creatures but after the traumatic experience in the club with people under masks resembling langurs when she meets the langur for the second time they seem to her like pierrots, clowns and bandits.

The animals and birds which are described in connection with Nanda are benign like domestic hens, houseflies or the animals of her imaginary world such as the Himalayan bear, crocodile or leopard. But Raka is described as a wild animal, "as secretive as a little wild bird, or an insect that hides." She is also compared to a jackal; "Raka no more needed or wanted, a house than a jackal did or a cicada. She was a wild creature—wild, wild, wild, thought Nanda Kaul" *(Fire on the Mountain* 103). Violence emerging out of the human world preys upon all the three major characters of this novel. Nanda Kaul is a victim of the violence of indifference of her husband, Ila Das is a victim of rape and murder, Raka is a victim of the world of her parent that she is born to. All the violence of the human world correspond to the violence in Nature that are expressed through the images of the hoopoes, the hen dragging out the worm, the destructive monkeys, snakes, night jars and jackals. Everything is engulfed by the forest fire at the end suggesting the "funeral fire," the fire of purgation:

> Lately her great-grandmother had bored her with it, played it with such theatrical ardour as to make it as unreal as theatre. It made her ache for the empty house on the charred hill, the empty summer-stricken view of the snakes, bones and smoldng kilns—all silent, and a forest fire to wipe it all away, leaving ashes and silence (120) [...]. (Das 212-16)

N.R. Gopal also subscribes to the view that Anita Desai uses symbols with strong thematic significance. In the chapter "Anita Desai's Fictional Techniques," Chapter Five of his book on Anita Desai, Gopal writes:

> *Fire on the Mountain* (1977) is a novel in which she makes use of symbolism. She also makes use of the flash back technique in narrating the story. The novel centres around the character of Nanda Kaul, the widow of vice-chancellor who is compelled both by choice and circumstances to live in seclusion in an old bunglow in Kasauli. The novel also makes use of fantasy and it is Nanda Kaul who lives in the world of fantasy. In order to engage attention of

her granddaughter Raka she spins several fantastic tales about her father. It is interesting to note that it is a grown-up person and not the child who goes into the world of fantasy. The use of fantasy in the novel has attracted critical attention and one of the critics has observed that Anita Desai has used fantasy not only in this novel but in her other novels too. This is how she has described the use of fantasy and various purposes for which it is used in the novel:

> [...] Self-revelation is not the main thrust of fantasy in *Fire on the Mountain* which uses it in an entirely different way. It is not bordering on hallucination. Two kinds of fantasy would exist side by side; one which is consciously and deliberately woven by Nanda Kaul to interest her great granddaughter Raka, the other which is shared by Raka and Ram Lal and is based on his belief in the supernatural [...]. Raka's private world of Fantasy is somewhere between the two—it is neither wholly and naturally accepted fact as the *Churails* are for Ram Lal, nor is it a lie woven for self-preservation— In *Fire on the Mountain,* fantasy also exists purely at the level of imagery as a part of the self analysis which some of the characters carry on." (Jain 47-51) (Gopal 84-85)

And again Gopal highlights Desai's use of symbols from wild nature in order to project Raka's temperament and behaviour:

We also come across the use of nature symbolism and imagery of wild nature in the context of Raka's character who is emotionally deprived and comes from a broken home. She is an unnatural child not interested in the fantastic tales of Nanda Kaul and she usually keeps her to herself. She is attracted towards the unpleasant aspects of nature like, the barren spaces of the valley. This attraction is an extemalisation of her sub-normal nature. The cosy-civilised world does not attract her, rather it is the uncompromising and lawless nature that pulls her:

> This hill, with its one destroyed house and one inbuilt one, on the ridge under the fire-singed pines, appealed to Raka with the strength of a strong sea-current—pulling, dragging. There was something about it—illegitimate, uncompromising and lawless—that made her tingle. The scene of devastation and failure somehow drew

> her, inspired her [-...]. It was the ravaged, destroyed and barren spaces in Kasauli that drew her: the ravine where yellow snakes slept under grey rocks and agaves growing out of the dust and rubble, the skeletal pines that rattled in the wind, the wind-levelled hill-tops and the seared remains of the safe, cosy, civilised world in which Raka had no part and to which she owed no attachment." (90-91)

Here nature imagery is a device to portray the character of Raka. Since she is deprived of parental love, she finds no interest in family or society. She finds more solace and interest in nature and that too in her wilder mood. Like the untamed lawless nature she too is stubborn and does not bother about her *Nani.* All the efforts on Nanda Kaul's part fail to interest her. The parallel between the untamed nature and her abnormal behaviour which culminates in her setting the mountain on fire is made clear when one day after her usual ramblings in the forest she comes back to "carignano," the bunglow where Nanda Kaul lives, chanting under her breath definitely and inaudibly, "I don't care—I don't care—I don't care for anything." The barren nature that attracts her is suggestive of emotionally barren family background from which she comes.

As in other novels in *Fire on the Mountain* too Anita Desai uses poetry and this time it is a poem by G.M. Hopkins. Although here the use of poem is not so significant yet it has some connection with the character of Nanda Kaul who quotes if and the poem signifies her desire to be away from humdrum of life, to a heaven of nature far from the madding crowd.

After quoting the poem it is explained that the poem is not about a geographical location but it is about a Nun's vocation, "but, all the same, it seemed to apply." And this is the poem:

> I have desired to go
> Where springs not fail,
> To fields where flies no sharp and sided hail
> And a few lilies blow,
> And I have asked to be
> Where no storms come,
> Where the green swell is in the havens dumb,

And out of the swing of the sea (58) [...].

(Gopal 86-87)

In the chapter, "Form and Structure," Chapter Five of her book on Anita Desai's style, Mohini Chakranarayan remarks:

In *Fire on the Mountain,* the self-destructive fire in the heart and mind of Nanda Kaul, juxtaposed with the bare physical surroundings caused by forest fires, decides the lyrical point of view.

[...] he stopped and kept behind while Nanda Kaul, slit-eyed burned on the knoll. *(Fire on the Mountain* 5)

The poetic design consists of Nanda Kaul a recluse by circumstance, Raka, a recluse by choice, and Ila Das a born recluse, because of her physical handicaps.

The setting is the symbolic house, called Carignano, which stands alone on a knoll, a meeting place for the three protagonists. The sets are combined both by explicit statements and implicit imagery. Only one more figure interacts with the three main protagonists, that is Ram Lal. This sparseness of characters, matches with the sparseness in vegetation.

Nanda Kaul is the passive purveyor of visions, who had chosen the house to find rest and relief from the mad world of duties and obligations. Through her, the poet narrator makes explicit her poetic vision. Nanda Kaul, as the symbolic hero, distorts the world in order to create an aesthetic image.

It was the place, and the time of life, that she had wanted and prepared for all her life. (3)

What pleased and satisfied her so, here at Carignano, was its barrenness. This was the chief virtue of all Kasauli of course—its starkness. (4)

Kasauli, a hill station, is presented as a barren, dry, unattractive place, surrounded by scenes of past and present forest fires, and always threatened with a new one. Nanda Kaul's choice of a house, at such a place, becomes the focal point of this dry and burnt landscape, which in fact, symbolises the inner self of the protagonist. A certain ambiguity of purpose prevails, which is again a characteristic of lyrical novels. This ambiguity is caused by ironical tones adopted to depict the conflict, between the real and the fleeing, escaping self of Nanda Kaul. Nanda Kaul wishes to break up with the past, but the past continuously impinges on her privacy and distracts her vision.

The protagonist's quest is represented symbolically by a lyrical progression, produced by elaborate picture scenes. The whole novel is interspersed with references to the past, in the form of the history of Carignano, life at Nanda Raul's husband, the vice-chancellor's house, scenes from Nanda Raul's childhood, history of Raka's parents, the history of Ila Das.

The present is mainly represented by Raka, her exploits and adventures, in direct juxtaposition with the experiences of Nanda Raul and Ila Das, who are three generations removed from her.

The concept of subjective objectivity followed by Anita Desai is present in this novel also. The experiences of Nanda Raul, who is in search of a total self, are arranged in a pattern of imagery. This pattern includes both human beings and objects, and are manifestations of the acting thought. Prominent images include Carignano—for seclusion, Rasauli— barrenness, starkness; History of Carignano—the loneliness misery of life, especially of lonely and unmarried women; Postman—animal existence; school boy—life of instincts; Ram Lal—servant endowed with a kind and gentle heart; life of Tara—failure of social life; and life at Vice Chancellor's house- duties and obligations; appearances; letters, messages, telephones—the outside world with which Nanda Raul wished to have no connection; eagle—Nanda Raul's aspirations for attaining higher self, the club-vanity and hollowness of a life of appearances; insects, lizards, crickets, cicadas—low self-esteem for herself and Raka; the climb to the monkey point— difference in age.

These are but a few listed. A single image may symbolise many things at the same time.

Raka is the catalyst in this novel. She leads Nanda Raul to the discovery of truth. In a lyrical novel, the protagonists wear the mask of the poet narrator. For the purpose of dramatic juxtaposition, the hero detaches himself from the scene of action, absorbs the action, and through the process of perception, mirrors it to create an ideal world.

Here in this novel, Nanda Kaul is only an observer, while Raka enacts the moral point of view in symbolic gestures. Raka does not change herself because:

> If Nanda Kaul was a recluse out of vengeance for a long life of duty and obligations her great-granddaughter was a recluse by nature, by instinct she had not arrived at the condition by a long route of rejection and sacrifice, she was born to it simply. (48)

Raka is often referred to as an insect, a cricket, a pet insect (39, 42, 45 and 54), which suggest that she was completely at home with nature. Unlike Nanda Kaul, she does not dream of orchards in Kashmir (93), but is happy to indulge in the hallucination of becoming a shipwrecked hero.

> I'm shipwrecked, Raka exulted. I'm shipwrecked and alone. She clung to a rock—my boat, alone in my boat on the sea, she sang. (61)

If Nanda Kaul's quest for ideal self-spelt calm and peace, for Raka it was complete oneness with the elements of nature. She is ecstatic to set the forest on fire. It is doubtful whether she was left unscathed.

> There was a scratching at the window that turned to a tapping, then a drumming, Nani, Nani, whispered Raka, shivering and crouching in the lily-bed peeping over the sill. Look Nani, I have set the forest on fire. (145)

This novel is the story of two persons. As Freedman says, 'The relationship of the double to its symbolic form is particularly vivid in those prose poems whose narrative movement draws attention to character and situation.'

While Nanda Kaul is full of contradictions, Raka is completely devoid of them. Unlike Nanda Kaul, who discovers her life as a lie (145) in the end, Raka has no compunctions. Nanda Kaul feels she is independent at Carignano, but gradually becomes emotionally dependent on Raka.

> But now Nanda Kaul seemed unwilling to stop talking, to let Raka out of her sight. There she flopped on her chair a small fish gasping for its native air but the old lady had her on the hook—a sharp bright hook—and held the string tight. (94-95)

Raka's presence is instrumental in bringing about the spiritual awakening in Nanda Kaul. Prior to her confessing being a liar, and her life a lie, she is filled with concern for everyone and everything around her.

> She well and strong and upright, she ought to protect her.
> She ought to fight some of the battles. (133)

By rejecting others, Nanda Kaul was rejecting herself. The recognition of her need for Raka, brings about the spiritual awareness which lends her the calm and serenity she was seeking all her life. Her protectiveness for the insect reveals it.

> Then becoming aware of Nanda Kaul's opaline presence, it lifted itself up on to its hind legs, as if in self-defence, and raised its tiny hands together under its chin, turning its solemn head from side to side as it studied her with exactly the same serene curiosity that marked her face.
>
> She put out her ringed hand and gave the lily a litde shake, so that the creature tumbled off into the leaves. There it would be safe from birds. (134)

The encounters of Nanda Kaul with Raka and Ila Das not only determine the movement of the novel, but form the symbolic self-portrait of her ideal self. The recognition of her need for others, the craving for love and belongingness is the fire of the spirit which purges her and forces the confession out of her [...] (Chakranarayan 95-98).

7

Narrative Technique

Story Within Story: Fantasy or Memory-making

Story within story is an age-old device which has been used by authors and narrators across space and time. In *Fire on the Mountain* Anita Desai uses it as a subtle narrative strategy, which reveals much about the teller and at the same time highlights the fictionality of the fiction thus created. At one point in the novel Nanda Kaul feels the need of some delusion. When Raka wants to know about her mother and she gives away the bare information that her mother is ill in nursing home again, Nanda is immediately repentant.

> In the silence that followed, Nanda Kaul bitterly cursed her failure to comfort children, her total inability to place herself in another's position and act accordingly. Fantasy and fairy tales had their place in life, she knew it so well. Why then did she tell the child the truth? Who wanted the truth? Who could stand it? Nobody. Not even herself. So how could Raka? (89)

This interior monologue of Nanda Kaul carries a clue to her own stories that she spins for Raka during the long rainy days in Carignano. It all started like this. As Raka stroked the little bronze Buddha on the table top, Nanda Kaul suddenly begins "in a high, musical voice that did not sound as if it belonged to her" (82):

> Isn't it a beautiful piece? [...] It comes all the way from Tibet, you know. My father brought it. (82)

Raka is surprised into attention, and Nanda Kaul continues to unroll her "scroll"; she goes on spinning a story about an explorer father. It is a story of splendour and glamour.

> That was long, long ago at a time when hardly anyone had even thought of trying to go to Tibet. [...] But my father [...] went as an explorer, out of curiosity [...]. We had spent the summer in Kashmir, of course. [...] It seemed we were travelling in paradise with him. But one morning, when we had camped beside a river of green ice water in a meadow that seemed untouched by a single foot-print, and the sky seemed the purest, cleanest sky there's ever been, he got onto his horse, Suleiman, dressed in fur and leather, and rode away over the pass, leaving us behind.
>
> He was away in Tibet—oh, for years, years. He went every step of the way on horseback, or on foot. The Mustagh Pass, the Baltoro glacier, the Aghil Pass [...] a terribly hard, dangerous route. (83)

As she weaves the story she talks "nervously," and "her voice rose unnaturally." Still, one must admit, she tells her story, created extempore as it is, superbly. She seems to have been carried away by her own imagination as she goes on composing the story of an 'explorer' father.

He traveled all over Tibet, had the strangest experiences. He spent nights in tiger-infested bamboo forests [...]. He joined in their famous archery competitions [...]. He went hunting with them, sometimes with falcons and sometimes with packs of dogs that were as large as asses, for musk deer [...]. On river banks, he saw them hunt for crocodiles [...]. Oh, he ate it too, and drank hot rice wine with them [...].

He bought Tibetan horses with clipped tails and rode them as they did—with stirrups long enough to stand up in so he could shoot his arrows from horseback. Horsemanship was most highly regarded all over Tibet, and then sports of the chase. Fortunately, he was good at both.

He went to Lhasa, saw the Potala. There he collected scrolls, bronzes, carpets—[...] and there he ran into [...] sorcerers [...] he told us he saw how darkness could fall at midday [...] till the sorcerer [...] made it vanish [...].

> He was an explorer, a discoverer. He traveled, hunted, collected exquisite things that he eventually brought home to us. (83-85)

Still there remain some visible pores in the story about which

Nanda is a bit uneasy, and therefore she tries to cover them up. Thus, immediately after mentioning his 'exquisite collections' Nanda realizes how bare the walls of Carignano look, and hastily adds:

> It is a pity I have none, or only so few, of his belongings. We were a large family—they were scattered [...]. And my sisters were all great collectors. (85)

So, she has only the Buddha.

However, once she has started to make it Nanda cannot stop. She starts constructing another house which could pride itself of all sorts of collections. But even as she describes the splendour of the house she herself seems to have been "dazzled" by her own imagination.

Again, she would invent a childhood in Kashmir, highlighting the exquisite delights of those days, including rowing in the lakes, putting up in the houseboats, fishing, riding, picking cherries, having picnic in shikaras, having tea on the lawns beside the fountains, etc. She also underscores the exotic beauty and charm of the unique house her father had provided them. The idyllic garden with its luxurious abundance of almonds and walnuts, pistachio and chilgoza, mushrooms, apricot and raisins, as well as the interior of the house, with all its profusion and pets,—the animals and birds—are indeed too good to be true.

As she tells these stories Raka cannot altogether ignore the charm, but she is "a bit suspicious" (95) nevertheless. As Nanda mentions her father's "private zoo" Raka glances at her—"a bit suspiciously but still, her eyes gave that flick of interest as of a fish wheeling around as it spotted bait" (95). And once Nanda has started the game she cannot stop.

> New as she was to the game, she was becoming an adept, she had a talent, she saw, for giving the child a slide-show, coloured and erratic. One slide would appear upside-down, or there would be a whole series that fluttered past too rapidly to be seen, but now and then one appeared steady, glowing and riveting and then Nanda Kaul straightened up with pride. (90)

Nanda Kaul rambles on "with an unaccustomed lightness and dreaminess of tone" (96).

Nanda Kaul projects idyllic heroic images of her husband and father. In her 'reminiscing' her husband appears to be a doting father who "loved to go riding with the children" (99) around the campus for miles, who "got up for the children [...] a badminton court, and we'd have such games out on the lawn, all of us, at times even by moonlight"; and "we could have anything we wanted of him, anything [...]" (100). As Nanda goes on valorizing her father, the 'explorer,' the 'collector,' the animal lover—"he admired anything uncommon, extraordinary [...]" (97)—Raka feels uneasy.

> She could not understand this new talkativeness of her great-grandmother's who had preferred, till lately, not to talk to her at all, nor had wanted to be talked to. Now she was unable to stop. (97)

Storytelling or fantasy-weaving has now gripped Nanda Kaul as a kind of compelling impulse which can be draining on whatever residual energy she still commands; it can be an indication of the approaching end or death as well. This is suggested by her occasional pauses—"with a start and a look of guilt, as if she had transgressed involuntarily and could not understand her own motive. If Raka had cared to notice, she would have seen a storm of disintegration cross that old, yellowed face with its intricate mapwork of fine lines [...]" (97).

But why does Nanda Kaul persist in her efforts to create the delusions which she herself knows not to be true? The author offers one explanation: "[...] now Nanda Kaul seemed unwilling [...] to let Raka out of her sight."

> She must not drive her away out of boredom or embarrassment. Somehow, she could not bear to let her slip away. It was as if Raka's indifference was a goad, a challenge to her [...]. (99)

Therefore she talks "in a flood [...] with a nervous animation and lightness that struck Raka's ear with a false note" (99).

When Ila Das comes to pay a visit to Nanda Kaul at Carignano, Nanda seems to hand over the job of story-telling or story-making to Ila Das. When Ila Das waxes eloquent on the subject of the 'Vice-Chancellor's house' Raka feels bored with "this tiresome tea-time game of old ladies [...] its cobweb maze. Lately her great-grandmother had bored her with it, played it with such theatrical ardour as to make it as unreal as theatre" (119-20). But today she perceives to her surprise that Nanda was not joining the game.

> It seemed Nanda Kaul had tired of her game. She was leaving it to Ila Das.
>
> Ila Das didn't mind. She didn't notice. (120)

Ila Das adds up to the story Nanda had already started during the long rains. She tries to evoke the grandeur and glitter of an ideal time in an ideal house, which extended welcome in all seasons, which was always full with happy children and pets, which offered music in winter and games in summer, and the elegant hostess presiding over it all. Even the melons in the garden were enormous, and lichee and jamun trees were loaded with ripe fruits (121).

But suddenly Nanda Kaul has dissociated herself from the game.

> She was not going to help Ila Das play this game. No, it was too shameful. She had decided that it was shameful and that, in any case, it had no appeal for Raka, the child who never played games. (121)

This seems to be in tune with the self-reflexive assertion in many a postmodern text about the status of narration as a sort of 'game.' Story-telling, the author seems to have been suggesting with a mild self-indulgent irony, can also be just another game, and the game has to be played according to its own rules: there must be two participants playing/performing their respective roles at the two ends,—the roles of the transmitter and the receiver respectively. In the absence or non-performance of either of the two, the game is bound to flop. When your listener loses interest then there is no point in spinning the yarn. In order to tell his story the 'Ancient Mariner' must have a 'wedding guest' to listen to him, and Nanda Kaul cannot play the ancient mariner to Raka for long, since the latter refuses to continue in the cast of the charmed 'wedding guest.'

The final disclosures, however, in the last page of the book come as a shocking reversal of all this myth-making. The great hiatus opens between, illusion, self-delusion and hard reality, as Ila Das turns to her friend "with a harsh honesty that was as real as her memory-making had been" (123).

Before long Nanda Kaul will admit the harsh reality about this memory-making.

> All those graces and glories with which she had tried to captivate Raka were only a fabrication: they helped her to sleep at night, they were tranquillizers, pills. She had lied to Raka. And Ila had lied, too. (145)

Thus the storytelling sessions of Nanda Kaul, to which Ila Das joins at a later stage, bring out the pathos behind the compulsive myth-making game of these two old friends, who have been left high and dry on the shores of life and time, and seek a little solace in weaving colourful fabrics of fantasy into the dry fibers of hard reality.

Ram Lal as Storyteller

Ram Lal also spins stories for Raka's entertainment. These are often macabre stories of ghosts, churails, mad dogs and mad foxes, or the mysterious workings of the doctors at the Pasteur Institute. These are also fabricated stories. But Ram Lal, while telling the stories almost believes them himself. The ghosts,—of man or dog—or the metamorphosis of a human into a rock are things not very unreal to his own imagination. Of course he exaggerates a bit in order to impress his child listener. Nevertheless he is an adept storyteller. And looking at them rapt in their conversation Nanda Kaul knows "Ram Lal could arouse Raka's interest and hold it as Nanda Kaul could not" (76).

Ram Lal is the traditional oral narrator with his inexhaustible source of wry anecdotes, and capacity for wild imaginings as well as of infecting his listeners with the same.

The interesting point to note in this connection is that all the story-tellers,—Nanda Kaul, Ila Das or Ram Lal—offer stories which are invariably larger than life; not one of them is strictly faithful to facts.

Nouvelle Form

According to Darshan Singh Maini,

> In *Fire on the Mountain* (1977) Anita Desai has further worked out and refined the nouvelle form which apparently suits her talents, imagination and style. For essentially, this three-character story does not admit of larger sociological or even philosophical variation. The framework, as usual, is skeletal in its rage and reach and reveals a new type of aesthetic asceticism evolved by the novelist in

> consonance with her endowments. The line of control and the line of vision remain close to each other, lending a felt intensity to this meager tale of two diminished and charred lives, and one counterpoint life of urgency, spontaneity and immediacy. I trust, this is probably Anita Desai's nearest brush with the Jamesian nouvelle, a form which the Master adored for its blessed deep-breathing economy. (132)

Time: The Fourth Dimension

In an interview with Sunil Sethi (December 1980) Anita observed that time was presented in her novel "as the fourth dimension of human existence." She says:

> My novel is about time as a destroyer, as a preserver and about what the bondage of time does to people. I have tried to tunnel under the mundane surface of domesticity.

Language

As Meenakshi Mukherjee sums up Anita Desai's style:

> Her language is marked by three characteristics: sensuous richness, a high-strung sensitiveness and a love for the sound of words. *(The Twice-Born Fiction.* 1974: 189)

Shiv K. Kumar, on the other hand, has serious reservations about Anita's style. As he would say:

> It is just words, in tangled sentence-structures, forcing the reader into a sort of insensateness. (1982: 194)

Or,

> a senile, spinsterish sensibility lashing inanities into excitement. (1982:193)

But Darshan Singh Maini also observes that "words appear to have sensuous appeal for her, and she exults in the reach and power of her rhetoric" (1970: 230).

The language of Desai's novel is remarkably terse and evocative. It is often poetic, charged with an intensity of perception. In this connection we may recall what the author said to Magda Costa; whereas initially she looked for models in the writings of such canonical British writers as Jane Austen, Virginia Woolf, D.H. Lawrence, E.M. Forster, *et al.*, and subsequently discovered and revered the Russian writers, especially Chekhov, and Dostoevsky, finally she turned to poetry for model.

> It's more and more poetry that I use as a model. I'm more interested now in reading poetry than fiction. I think they use language in a way I would like to emulate. I would like to achieve that gravity, compression, the intensity of their language.

According to Iyengar, "Since her preoccupation is with the inner world of sensibility rather than the outer world of action, she has tried to forge a style supple and suggestive enough to convey the fever and fretfulness of the stream-of-consciousness of her principal characters."

Anita also makes the proud claim, "Language is the universal whore *whom* I have made a virgin." (Srivastava 216). We may also remember what the author herself told during the interview taken by Magda Costa:

> [when you write] you are alone with that page and with your pen. You are really only playing a game by yourself: of imagining thoughts and images with the best words suitable. It's an exploration of language: how much can language do, or how far can it pretend human experience and feelings.

These two assertions, taken together, suggest the degree of self-consciousness which apparently informs the prose style of Anita Desai.

By making linguistic analysis of the first page of *Fire on the Mountain* Chakranarayan has shown in her book *Style Studies in Anita Desai* how Desai's sentence structures, use of proper and common nouns, use of plosives and fricatives, use of words with pejorative meanings or passive connotations, careful use of different figures of speech, particularly metaphors, antitheses, zoological images, irony etc. contribute to and reinforce the thematic and structural patterns of the novel.

The Author on Her Art

The author is supposed to have said on an interview [Atma Ram, "An Interview with Anita Desai," *World Literature Written in English.* April 1977]:

> A writer does not create a novel by observing a given set of theories [...] he follows flashes of individual vision, and relies on a kind of instinct that tells him what to follow and what to avoid, how to veer away from what would

> be destructive to his vision. It is these flashes of vision, and a kind of trained instinct that leads him [...] not any theories.

In the same interview the author had stressed a distinction between writers along the gender line:

> [Women] live mostly in such confined spheres and therefore their field of observation is at the same time more restricted and more intense. This leads to their placing their emphasis differently from men, on having a very different sense of values. Whereas a man is concerned with action, experiences and achievement, a woman writer is more concerned with thought, emotion and sensation.

In an interview with Dalmia Yashodhara (in 1979) the author half-jokingly commented on her writing as a kind of obsession.

> It has become such a deeply ingrained habit, it is like chain-smoking. I chain smoke with words, with books. There is a difference, of course; what begins as a self-indulgence eventually becomes a self-discipline.

The process of creativity has been regarded by the author as simultaneously obsessive and disciplining. A novel, according to her, would grow in the mind,

> As silently and unobtrusively as a grain of sand enters a shell. There it grows and develops [...]. Eventually this tiny grain grows into such a mass that it begins to exert pressure. (Srivastava 214)

At the same time,

> The process of rewriting did, however, bring in the disciplinary power of discrimination and criticism and wrought further changes. (Srivastava 216)

This discipline is reflected in her handling of the form of fiction. It is remarkable how she has absorbed all sorts of influences and assimilated them in order to reach a unique vision and style. Desai herself has identified some of these influences on her. She recalls her experience of reading *Wuthering Heights* for the first time.

> It struck me with the force of a gale and I still vibrate to it. Ever since, literature has seemed to me more interesting, more significant and more overwhelming than the real world. Late, of course, other writers meant more to me.

> In my twenties when I first began to work seriously and consciously on my novels, it was D.H. Lawrence, Virginia Woolf, Henry James and Proust who influenced me more strongly.
>
> [Cited by R.K. Srivastava, *Perspectives on Anita Desai.* 217]

Incidentally, all these masters are noted for their intensity of imagination and expression, which is also the hallmark of Anita's writings.

She also shows the sensitive writer's sense of delicacy and sanctimony regarding her own art. As she puts it:

> I confess I am afraid of speaking out about the art of writing, the mechanics of my craft. I have an intuitive and deep fear that by speaking of something subterranean and subconscious, I will destroy it—it is something very frail.
>
> [Cited by R.K. Dhawan. *The Fiction of Anita Desai.* 10]

Critical Responses

In course of discussing the novels of Anita Desai in terms of style **Mohini Chakranarayan** refers to the idea of discourse as suggested by Leech and Short in *Style in Fiction* (1970); in the Fourth Chapter, "Rhetoric of the Novels of Anita Desai," of her book on Anita Desai's style, Chakranarayan argues:

> Discourse means 'linguistic communication' seen as transaction between speaker and hearer, in prose fiction it is the author and the reader.
>
> Discourse in prose fiction also has an extended meaning of rapport between the writer and the reader.
>
> Every writer assumes that he shares a common fund of knowledge and experience with his readers. This general background not only consists of common facts but also knowledge of historical events, literary works and even quotations from the latter. Because the author can assume knowledge which any particular reader might not necessarily have, we have to conclude that the addressee in literary communication is not the reader, but what may be more conveniently termed as the implied reader, a hypothetical personage who shares with the author not just background knowledge but also a set of

> presuppositions, sympathies and standards of what is pleasant and unpleasant, good and bad, right and wrong.

In keeping with the term 'implied reader,' Booth has used the term 'implied author.'

> It is a curious fact that we have no terms either for this created second self or for our relationship with him. None of our terms for various aspects of the narrator is quite accurate. 'Persona,' 'mask' and 'narrator' are sometimes used but they more commonly refer to the speaker in the work who is after all only one of the elements created by the implied author and who may be separated from him by large ironies. Narrator is usually taken to mean the 'I' of the work but the T is seldom if ever identical with the implied image of the artist.

> In other words the views expressed in a writing cannot be automatically ascribed to the author. The arrangement may be arbitrary according to the needs of artistic arrangement. Booth further adds:

> Some aspects of the implied author may be inferred through tonal variations, but his major qualities will depend also on hard facts of action and character in the tale that is told. The 'implied' author chooses, consciously or unconsciously what we read, we infer him as an ideal literary created version of the real man; he is the sum of his own choices.

Viewed from this angle, the novels of Anita Desai reveal interesting information about their implied authors [...].

> In *Fire on the Mountain,* the author's voice is in direct juxtaposition to that of Nanda Kaul. The author narrates and interprets at the same time. The evaluative terms and inferences, ironic contrast and reversal and rhetorical questions, all very prominent in this writing, highlight the irony of tone. This irony of tone is coupled with irony of fate which mellows Nanda Kaul's personality and allows the reader to penetrate her inner self, which is hill of longings for love and companionship. Authorial voice changes from scene to scene. Raka and Ila Das are described in impersonal tones with complete objectivity,

while Nanda Kaul engages the mind of the author. Towards the end, the voices of Nanda Kaul and the author merge in the confession of Nanda Kaul.

The tone of ironic disapproval gradually changes to tacit agreement, and finally to sympathy towards the end. Once the reader is informed about the neglect and rebuff suffered by Nanda Kaul, he no longer considers her a brutal snob but becomes tolerant of her ideology, and in the end he is left with feelings of regret for the irretrievable [...] (Chakranarayan 109-24).

8

The Novel as Feminist Discourse

We can start this part of our discussion with a quotation from Adrienne Rich:

> I think that every feminist poet must long—I do—for real criticism of her work—not just descriptive, but analytic criticism which takes her language and images seriously enough to question them [...] it would be better for all feminist writers if such principled criticism were to come also from strangers—it would broaden the field in which we are working.
>
> (Adrienne Rich, "Toward a More Feminist Criticism." *Blood, Bread and Poetry: Selected Prose 1978-1985.* London: Virago, 1987: 91)

Michael Ryan in his usual, which is wonderfully transparent, style introduces 'Feminism,' the loaded term, in the following manner

> Feminism asks why women have played a subordinate role to men in human societies. It is concerned with how women's lives have changed throughout history, and it asks what about women's experience is different from men's, either as a result of an essential ontological or psychological difference or as a result of historical imprinting and social construction. Feminist literary criticism studies literature by women for how it addresses or expresses the particularity of women's lives and experience. And it studies the male-dominated canon in order to understand how men have used culture to further their domination of women. (Ryan 101)

Since 1969, there has been an explosion of feminist writings. To use Elaine Showalter's metaphor, the movement displays the urgency and excitement of a religious awakening. Again, it is not a unitary theory of procedure, but rather accommodates a variety of critical vantage points.

At the same time, however, there is also some common ground, which constitutes of a basic perception of the factor of sexual discrimination and difference. One of the most dominant of these common assumptions is that civilization, as perceived by the feminists, has been pervasively patriarchal, male-oriented, and controlled by the male; it has been consistently organized and conducted in such a way as to subordinate women to men in all cultural domains: familial, religious, political, economic, social, legal, and artistic. The point of reference all along has been man; woman is negative,—non-man, Other. Women are also made to internalize the patriarchal ideology, and thus actively co-operate in their own subjugation.

Secondly, the prevailing concepts of gender are cultural constructs. Beauvoir's famous utterance: "One is not born, but rather becomes, a woman [...]. It is civilization as a whole that produces this creature [...] which is described as feminine," operates at the heart-centre of feminist discourse/s.

Thirdly, it is an androcentric ideology that pervades all great literature written by male authors: *Oedipus, Ulysses, Hamlet, Tom Jones, Moby Dick,* etc. They lack the autonomous female role models, and leave the woman reader an alien outsider.

Thus the emphases of feminist discourse generally come to be laid on the following agenda:

(a) To alter the way a woman reads the literature of the past, so that she can resist the author's intentions & designs by a "revisionary re-reading" (Judith Fetterley's *The Resisting Reader* 1978);

(b) To identify recurrent "images of women" in literature by men, which are found to broadly follow two typical patterns—the innocent virgin or "angel in the house" (Coventry Patmore), who are the idealized projections of men's desire, and the Eve-Pandora-Delilah type, who are the demonic projections of man's sexual resentments and terrors;

(c) To address literary and cultural products from the perspective of gyno-criticism. Gynocriticism is Elaine Showalter's term to indicate a criticism that develops a specifically female framework for dealing with work written by women. Some of the noted figures in gynocriticism are Sandra Gilbert and Susan Guber *(The Madwoman in the Attic* 1979), Elain Showalter *(A Literature of their Own: British Women Novelists from Bronte to Lessing* 1977); Patricia Meyer Spacks *(The Female Imagination* 1975), *et al.*

(d) To identify the distinctively feminine subject matter in literature by women—gestation, giving birth, nurturing, mother-daughter relationship, for instance.

(e) To uncover in lit history a female tradition.—Elaine Showalter, *A Literature of their Own* (1977).

(f) To rearrange/re-order/displace the literary canon by raising the status of female authors ignored heretofore: Aphra Behn, for example.

In a sense feminism can be defined as a 'consciousness raising' movement *(a la* Adrienne Rich), as suggested by the following two definitions:

> Once grasped at a general level ideas become like a kind of shorthand in our consciousness. But it is one thing to encounter a concept, quite another to understand it. In order to understand a general idea like hegemony it is necessary first to perceive in a whole series of separate moments how this has affected you. Then those moments have to be communicated. This is part of the total process of female self-recognition. It is the way through which we start to make our own language, and discover our own reflections.
>
> (Sheila Rowbotham. *Woman's Consciousness, Man's World.* 1973: 39)

> Feminism is the first theory to emerge from those whose interest it affirms. Its method recapitulates as theory the reality it seeks to capture. As Marxist method is dialectical materialism, feminist method is consciousness raising: the collective critical reconstitution of the meaning of women's social experience, as women live through it.
>
> (MacKinnon, 'Feminism, Marxism, Method and the State.' O. Keoane, Rosaldo and Gelpi. *Feminist Theory: A Critique of Ideology.* 1982: 29)

The intensity of the emotional tenor of the movement can be felt particularly in the poetry of these writers. For instance let me cite a few lines from a poem by Ketaki Kushari Dyson:

I implore you,
all who read my lines,
if you have mothers,
sister, wives, or daughters,
remember those
who have been forced to pay
in the high-flated currency of pain
for being born women.
And should a woman
dare to speak out loud
about how she has been
mauled by love or hate,
suffer her to speak
Do not shut her up.

(Dyson, "After Reading Nawal El Saadawi's [...]"
Spaces l Inhabit. India: Navana, 1983)

Judith Fetterley, in her famous treatise—"On the Politics of Literature" (1978) registers some of the ambitious targets of feminism:

> Consciousness is power. To create a new understanding of our literature is to make possible a new effect of that literature on us. And to make possible a new effect is in turn to provide the conditions for changing the culture that the literature reflects. To expose and question that complex of ideas and mythologies about women and men which exist in our society and are confirmed in our literature is to make the system of power embodied in the literature open not only to discussion but even to change.

While admitting that such questioning and exposure can be carried on only by a consciousness radically different from the one that informs the literature, Judith Fetterley argues:

> Such a closed system cannot be opened up from without. It must be entered into from a point of view which questions its values and assumptions and which has its investment in making available to consciousness precisely

> that which the literature wishes to keep hidden. Feminist criticism provides that point of view and embodies that consciousness.

Feminism is, again, a project or a movement in which the writer and the critic have to join hands. As Sandra Gilbert and Susan Guber had enjoined the woman writer to do in their famous book, *The Madwoman in the Attic* (1980):

> [...] a woman writer must examine, assimilate, and transcend the extreme images of "angel" and "monster" which male authors have generated for her. Before we women can write, declared Virginia Woolf, we must "kill" the "angel in the house." In other words, women must kill the aesthetic ideal through which they themselves have been "killed" into art. And similarly all women writers must kill the angel's necessary opposite and double, the "monster" in the house, whose Medusa-face also kills female creativity.

Gilbert and Guber also simultaneously stresses the task of the feminist critic:

> For us as feminist critic, however, the Woolfian act of "killing" both angels and monsters must here begin with an understanding of the nature and origin of these images. At this point in our construction of a feminist poetics, then, we really must dissect in order to murder. And we must particularly do this in order to understand literature by women because, as we shall show, the images of "angel" and "monster" have been so ubiquitous throughout literature by men that they have also pervaded women's writing to such an extent that few women have definitively "killed" either figure.

Anita Desai has achieved that feat of "killing" both the figures in her depiction of Nanda Kaul in *Fire on the Mountain*. She has evoked both the paradigms and subtly subverted both in the superb portraiture of Nanda Kaul.

Molly Hite contends in her perceptive study of the impact of feministic discourse on innovative certain women writers of our times, *The Other Side of the Story* (1989):

> [...] a number of the most eminent and influential women writing in the contemporary period are attempting innovations in narrative form that are *more* radical in

> their implications than the dominant modes of fictional experiment, and more radical precisely inasmuch as the context for innovation is a critique of a culture and a literary tradition apprehended as profoundly masculinist. (Hite 2)

In this context Hite points out how these writers'—Hite's focus is Jean Rhys, Doris Lessing, Alice Walker, and Margaret Atwood—innovative strategies remain recognizably distinct from the masculinist writings of other contemporaries or postmodernists. While sharing the decentering strategies of postmodern narratives, "they seem to arrive at these strategies by an entirely different route, which involves emphasizing conventionally marginal characters and themes, in this way re-centering the value structure of the narrative" (Hite 2). As result we get the 'other side' of the story which had been relegated to invisibility or obscurity in masculinist writings since ages. This 'other side' of the story is also the story of the 'other woman,' the invisible, hidden woman behind the facade of patriarchal constructs.

In *Fire on the Mountain,* written during the first high tide of feminism in the West, Anita Desai allows us a glimpse of this 'other side' of the story of an Indian woman. She has attempted to trace the story of the 'other woman,' the individual Nanda, behind the glamorous facade of roles—Nanda Kaul, the Vice-Chancellor's exhibit wife, the dutiful daughter and daughter-in-law, the beautiful wife always in silk saree, the expert housewife, the caring mother, and what not. But these images of so-called grandeur or glamour are evoked only through flashback. The immediate focus is on something quite unusual—an old withered lady, living all by herself an isolated life in an isolated hilltop house—stiff, stem, rigid in her decisive attitude of withdrawal from society and people.

Such a figure can offer very little attraction for the romantically disposed young reader. It is not another "heroine's text," which were so common with the nineteenth century writers, irrespective of gender. In fact Nanda's life had been one long drab dull drudgery. It was a necessarily entrapped life. So, even when she gives free rein to her imagination she produces only a series of 'houses' or enclosures, however fantastic they may be made to look. Nanda Kaul's life had been an empty one, devoid of any fulfilling consciousness of a personal being and becoming. Thus the 'other side' of her story which is revealed in a series of flitting flashbacks, and finally captured in a frieze, shows how simple, how familiar, how common a story it was. The very simplicity or bareness of her life encapsulates the author's cultural critique of this life. As Simone de Beauvoir points out: "She is defined and differentiated with reference to man and not he with reference to her; she is the incidental, the inessential as opposed to the essential. He is the Subject, he is the Absolute—she is the Other." Through the story of Nanda Raid Anita Desai exposes and articulates the constraints and the banality of her situation which is symptomatic of the situation of many a Indian housewife. As Mamta Koila superbly sums up this crippling, nullifying situation in her poem "Anonymous":

> [...] You called me wife,
> I was taught to break saccharine in your tea and
> To offer at the right moment the vitamins. Cowering
> Beneath your monstrous ego I ate the magic loaf and
> Became a dwarf. Lost my will and reason, to all your
> Questions I mumbled incoherent replies.

We can also have a better understanding of Nanda's act of spinning 'stories' in the light of prevailing feminist discourse. These are the wishfid thinking, escape routes from the dull drabness of 'her' real life; at the same time these are also meant to cater to the conventional cultural constructs—an ideal and idolized father, a glamorous and loving/caring husband, who are the controlling 'subjects.' Desai makes this castle in the air come down with a crash, and thus exposes the non-viability of these traditional constructs. It is again, notable that even in the dream-houses Nanda never attains the centre stage. Just as in the real house of the real past she tiptoes on the fringes of the badminton court,—a space appropriated by other people to play other game/s—her dream- houses too get crowded with the masters' things, their collections, their animals. She is at the centre of only one house, Carignano.

Anita Desai focuses this marginal woman, who tells one set of narratives, and simultaneously/alternately recalls another set of memories. She would have repressed the latter. But still they would come back again and again, and compel the reader to hear the 'other side of an old, familiar story.'

In this context one is reminded of Anna, the writer protagonist of Doris Lessing's *The Golden Notebook* (New York: Bantam, 1981). Early in the narrative Anna feels disturbed about her own writing; she writes: "I am simply asking myself; Why a story at all [...]. Why not, simply, the truth?" (63). What Molly Hite observes in this connection is equally applicable to Nanda Kaul's predicament, the compulsion of her situation:

> [...] and this opposition, story versus truth, haunts her as one meaning of her inability to write and as a paradigm of the tendency of preexisting form to "block off" possibility in the same way that people "block off' parts of themselves in order to stay whole. (Hite 67)

At the same time, Nanda Kaul's myth-making—all of which revolve round various 'houses'—can be considered in the light of 'home' as an emerging paradigm in the feminist writing, a paradigm which is often embedded with ambivalence. For example, in Adrienne Rich's poetry we find a balanced ambivalence about home. It is often a conflict between a determined shelter and an indeterminate flight, between a private space and a public place. "Home becomes the site of a complicated struggle between the desire to return to a place of sheltered belonging and the desire to leave oppressive social structures" (Harriet Davidson 168). Nanda and Raka reenact between themselves these complex and conflicting desires regarding 'home.' A few lines from Rich's 1983 poem, "In the Wake of Home" may be cited in this connection.

> The family coil so twisted, tight and loose
> anyone trying to leave
> has to strafe the field
> burn the premises down

This immediately calls up Raka's final act from which the novel derives its title.

Like Adrienne Rich, Anita Desai also "would change the idea of home from a nostalgic vision hiding political reality to a real, material goal of security and comfort. [...] too often home is the least safe of places, too often the idea of home prevents us from finding the comfort we need. And yet home is also the site of speaking, the place of a shared language and of meaning, the place to find a voice to speak for those who have no home or voice. Rich [or Desai] will not leave home behind, but will keep it as a site of contradiction in a politics of location" (Harriet Davidson 176).

Again, in order to write about the 'other side' of the story of the 'other' woman the writers have to write in a new way, 'otherwise,' and thus like many a feminist writers of our times Anita Desai also eludes certain established modes of reading. While some critics express reservations, some bafflement, we should understand that she is writing or translating another side or dimension of realism. For example, if the narrative seems disjointed it is because it is meant to give the feel of the state of a mind of someone who has been precariously hanging on the verge of death or disintegration. If the language seems uneven,—sometimes lyrical, sometimes halting, sometimes exquisitely fine and appropriate, sometimes almost creaking under the pressure of crowded memories and associations—it is precisely carrying the genuine note of an interrupted, ruptured stream-of-consciousness, flowing out of a ruptured, mangled trickle which has constituted the life. In her inimitable way Charlotte Bronte had summed up the futility of this kind of life that the sexist cultural norms imposed upon women in *Jane Eyre* which has been called "a cult text of feminism" by Gayatri Spivak *(Critical Inquiry* 12). The passage has since been made famous by Virginia Woolfs citing in *A Room of One's Own*.

> Women are supposed to be very calm but women feel just as men feel; they need exercise for their faculties and a field for their efforts as much as their brothers do; they suffer from too rigid a restraint, too absolute a stagnation, precisely as men would suffer; and it is narrow-minded in their more privileged fellow-creatures to say that they ought to confine themselves to making puddings and knitting stockings, to playing on the piano and embroidered bags [...].

This applies equally to Nanda Kaul and Ila Das.

In *Fire on the Mountain* Anita Desai has subtly evoked certain paradigms which have enjoyed a kind of centrality in mainstream literature and culture, and then has finely subverted the same paradigms in course of the story. These are the paradigms of happy children, indulgent parents, happy wife and mother, big houses run by happy wives and ruled by wonderful god-like patriarchs. These have been foisted up only in order to be dismantled eventually. She invokes these paradigms only to show how empty they were, how false and unreal, and how exhausted of all meanings when seen from the 'other side of the story.'

The mountain emerges as a rich symbol of this isolating and estranging version of the 'other.'

It is perhaps interesting to note that in spite of all the attempts of various people at devising 'stories' at different points in the novel, there is actually not much of a story as such. This is also a feature of feminism-oriented fiction. As LeAnne Schreiber observes about Margaret Atwood's *Lady Oracle:*

> The novel does not develop, it meanders, circling around and turning on itself—letting its contours be defined by the chaos of the heroine's psyche. *(Time.* 11 October 1976: 98)

The narrative course of *Fire on the Mountain* can also be charted along this circuitous repetitive curve as its contours are defined by the chaos of the heroine's psyche.

Fire on the Mountain is basically a story of women. In addition to the central figures,—Nanda Kaul, Raka, Ila Das— the periphery too accommodates women figures like Tara, the shattered wife, or the girl child whom Ila Das would have saved from a horrible marriage, or Ila Das's handicapped yet brave sister Rima, and their invalid mother whom Rima looks after, or the old woman who had gone mad after her hill-top cottage house had burnt down in the forest fire, or the hapless poor women in the hamlets of the valley, compared to whom even Ila Das feels herself to be in a better position. We do not see them on the immediate stage, we do not hear them, but they are around as silent presences, and one can, as it were, feel the pulsation of their suffering beating through the story. The centre-stage, that is Carignano, brings together three women who are foregrounded against this backdrop of a silent still house and an evoked crowd of silent sad women. The trio of Nanda-Ila-Raka are again mutually contrastive. Nanda and Ila are opposite to each other in appearance, bearing, life pattern, past experience, in short almost everything under the sun. Again, Raka represents a counterpoint to the two ladies: Raka is a child, whereas Nanda and Ila are quite old, old enough to be a great-grandmother. At the same time it is, significantly, a matrilinear line that ties Raka to Nanda, whereas Nanda and Ila have been bound to each other by inseverable bond of countless shared memories of grief and humiliation. Ryan's observation on the projection of women's relationship in feminist writing seems enlightening in the present context:

> Many works of literature are feminist not because they criticize the pathologies of patriarchy but because they offer images of women forming supportive communities or relationships that can enable either the struggle to make a post-patriarchal world or the attempt to survive within the patriarchy. (Ryan 114)

This is the bond that ties the two old friends and the child together in Desai's novel. Here we can cite from a poem by Gauri Deshpande, which seems so very relevant in the context of these sororist and matrilinear relationships.

> Sometimes you want to talk
> about love and despair
> and the ungratefulness of children.
> A man is no use whatsoever then.
> You want then your mother
> or sister
> or the girl with whom you went through school,
> and your first love, and her
> first child—a girl—
> and your second.
> You sit with them and talk
> She sews and you sit and sip
> and speak of the rate of tea
> and the scarcity of cheese.
> You both know that you've spoken
> of love and despair and ungratified children.
>
> ("The Female of the Species")

Sample Questions

1. Analyse and comment on the author's description of Carignano, and bring out its thematic significance in the novel.
2. Examine Desai's use of 'Houses' as a powerful motif in the novel.
3. Consider Desai's use of the 'mountain' as a trope.
4. Discuss the elaborate pattern of symbols in the novel.
5. Examine the 'stories within the story' and comment on their thematic/artistic significance.
6. Examine the view that *Fire on the Mountain* is the story of women.
7. Analyse and comment on the ending of the novel.

Short Questions

1. What is Nanda's feeling at the approach of the postman? Why does she feel so?
2. Who are the successive owners of Carignano?
3. What are the two houses that attract Raka most, and why?
4. There is a reference to a poem by Hopkins. Cite the reference and locate the context.
5. Identify the allusion in the title. How does the allusion apply in the present context?
6. Why does Raka come to Carignano?
7. When and why does Nanda start telling stories? Who is her auditor?
8. What happens to Ila Das at the end?

Bibliography

A. PRIMARY SOURCES

(i) Novels

Cry, the Peacock. London: Peter Owen Ltd., 1963. Calcutta: Rupa & Co., 1964.

Voices in the City. London: Peter Owen, 1965. Delhi: Hind Pocket Books, 1968.

Bye-Bye, Blackbird. Delhi: Hind Pocket Books, 1971.

Where Shall We Go This Summer? Delhi: Vikas Publishing House, 1975.

Fire on the Mountain. London: William Heinemann, 1977. New York: Harper & Row, 1977. Delhi: Allied Publishers, 1977. *Clear Light of Day.* London: William Heinemann, 1980. New York: Harper & Row, 1980. New Delhi: Allied Publishers, 1980.

The Village By the Sea. London: William Heinemann, 1982.

Delhi: Allied Publishers, 1983. (Novel for Children).

In Custody. London: William Heinemann, 1984.

Baumgartner's Bombay. London: Heinemann, 1988.

Journey to Ithaca. London: Heinemann, 1995.

For Children

The Peacock Garden. Bombay: Indian Book House, 1974.

London: William Heinemann, 1979.

Cat on a House Boat. Bombay: Orient Longman, 1976.

The Village by the Sea. London: William Heinemann, 1982. Delhi: Allied Publishers, 1983.

(ii) Short Stories

Games at Twilight. London: William Heinemann, 1978. Bombay: Allied Publishers, 1978. New York: Harper and Row, 1980. Sweden: Trivi, 1980. Harmondsworth: Penguin Books, 1982.

(iii) Non-Fiction

"Calcutta Kaleidoscope." *Illustrated Weekly of India,* 1958. "Gangtok." *Envoy* (London), 1959.

"A Kulu Christmas." *Envoy* (London), 1959.

"Pilgrimage." Illustrated Weekly of India, *1966.*

"Women Writers." *Quest* 65, Apr.-June 1970: 39-43.

"Book I Enjoyed Writing Most." *Contemporary Indian Literature* 13.4 (1973): 23-24.

"The Indian Writer's Problems." *Literary Criterion* 12.4 (1975): 26-26. Also in *ACLALS Bulletin* 4th Ser. No. 2 (1975): 12-14. "Jhabvala: A Sure Winner." *Illustrated Weekly of India 7* Mar. 1976: 6.

"Within and Without Tradition." *ACLALS Newsletter* 5 Apr. 1979: 5-21.

"Literary Lapses." *Book Review.* July-Aug. 1982: 8-10. "Contemporary English Literature in India." *Littcrit* 14, 8.1: 65-68.

"Flight of Forms." India International Centre Quarterly *10.4* : 419.

"Out of the Shadows." *Indian Express* 10 June 1984: 5. "Indian Fiction Today." *Deadalus* 118 (1989): 207-231.

"The Rage for the Raj." *New Republic* 25 Nov. 1985.

"A Secret Connivance." *Times Literary Supplement* 14 Sept. 1990.

(iv) Reviews

Memoirs of Mendicant Professor: A Review. Quest *July-Aug. 1970*

Rev. of Hymns in Darkness. Indian P.E.N. *Mar.-Apr. 1977: 3-4.*

"Where Culture Clash by Night." Rev. of *Midnight's Children* by Salman Rushdie. *Washington Post* 15 May 1981. 1, 13. 'Book World.'

"An Oriental Fantasy." Rev. of *Midnight's Children* by Salman Rushdie. *Book Review* July-Aug. 1981: 23-26.

"Timeless Tales." Rev. of Narayan's *Under the Banayan Tree and Other Stories. India Today* 16 Nov. 1985. 152-153.

"Narayan's Country." Rev. of *Malgudi Days. New York Times Books Review* 7 Mar. 1982: 1.

"Inner Sphere." Rev. of *The Circle of Reason* by Amitav Ghosh. *India Today,* 15 Mar. 1986: 149.

(v) Interviews

Banerjee, Purabi. "Bookworm's Progress." An Interview with Anita Desai. *Statesman* 10 Apr. 1983: 3.

Bliss, Corinne. "Against the Current: A Conversation with Anita Desai." *Massachusetts Review* 29.3 (1988): 521-537.

Dalmia, Yashodhara. An Interview with Anita Desai. *Times of India* 29 Aug. 1979: 13.

Ferrell, Sarah. "A Banquet of Language." A Telephonic Interview. *New York Times Book Review* 9 Apr. 1989: 3.

H.K. "Where Are the Errors." Interview with Anita Desai. *Hindustan Times* 20 Nov. 1983:

Jain, Jasbir. Interview with Anita Desai. *Rajasthan University Studies in English* 12 (1979): 61-69.

Libert, Florence. An Interview with Anita Desai. 1 Aug., 1985. Published in *World Literature Written in English* 30.1 (1990): 47-55.

Petersen, Kirsten Holst. Interview with Anita Desai. *Kunapipi* 6.3 (1984): 83-85.

Ram, Atma. An Interview with Anita Desai. *World Literature Written in English* 16.1 (1977): 95-104.

—"Anita Desai: The Novelist Who Writes for Herself." Interview with Anita Desai. *Journal of Indian Writing in English* 5.2 (1977): 39-42.

—Interview with Anita Desai. *Journal of Indian Writing in English* 5.2 (1977): 39-42

—An Interview with Anita Desai. *Morality in Tess and Other Essays*. New Delhi: Mittal Publications: 1996: 96-99.

Replies to the Questionnaire by Anita Desai. *Kakatiya Journal of English Studies* 3.1 (1978): 1-16.

Robinson, Andrew. Interview with Anita Desai. *Saturday Statesman*. 13 Aug. 1988.

Ray, Madhushree Sinha. "Silent Spaces of Inner Vastness: Meet the Author." *Times of India* 18 June 1992: 7.

Sethi, Sunil. "Tremendous Changes." Interview with Anita Desai. *India Today* Dec. 1-15, 1980: 142-143.

Seguet, Pascale. An interview with Anita Desai. *Commonwealth Essays and Studies* (France) 10.2 (1988): 40-50.

Sheth, Ketaki. "It's Fatal to Write with an Audience in Mind." Interview with Anita Desai. *Imprint* June 1984.

Srivastava, Ramesh K. "Anita Desai at Work: An Interview." *Perspectives on Anita Desai.* Ed. Ramesh K. Srivastava. Ghaziabad: Vimal Prakashan, 1984. 208-26.

B. SECONDARY SOURCES: CRITICAL WORKS

(i) Bibiliographies

Bande, Usha. "Bibliography." *The Novels of Anita Desai.* New Delhi: Prestige Books, 1988. 177-88.

Dash, Sandhyarani. "Bibliography." *Form and Vision in the Novels of Anita Desai.* New Delhi: Prestige Books, 1996. 87-94.

Goel, Kunj Bala. "Bibliography." *Language and Theme in Anita Desai's Fiction.* Jaipur: Classical Publishing House, 1989. 179-190.

Gopal, N. R. "Bibliography." *A Critical Study of the Novels of Desai.* New Delhi: Atlantic Publishers, 1995. 103-114. Indira, S. "Bibliography." *Anita Desai as an Artist. A Study in Image and Symbol.* New Delhi: Creative Books, 1994. 200-211.

Jain, Jasbir. "Bibliography." *Stairs to the Attic: The Novels of Anita Desai.* Jaipur: Printwell Publishers, 1987. 161-172.

Khanna, Shashi. "Select Bibliography." *Human Relationships in Anita Desai Novels.* New Delhi: Sarup and Sons. 1995. 135-150.

Narendra Kumar, V.L.V.N. "Bibliography." *Fits and Misfits: A Study of Anita Desai's Protagonists.* Bareilly: Prakash Book Depot, 1995-96. 90-100.

Pathania, Usha. "Bibliography." Human Bonds and Bondages: The Fiction of Anita Desai and Kamala Markandaya. *Delhi: Kanishka Publishing House, 1992.*

Ram, Atma, Comp. "Anita Desai: A Bibliography." *Journal of Indian Writing in English* 9.1 (1981): 93-98.

Sharma, Kajali. "Bibliography." *Symbolism in Anita Desai's Novels.* New Delhi: Abhinav Publications, 1991. 166-174.

Srivastava, Ramesh K., Comp. "Anita Desai: Selected Bibliographies." *Six Indian Novelists in English.* Amritsar: Guru Nanak Dev University, 1987. 346-351.

Tripathy, J.P. "Bibliography." *The Mind and Art of Anita Desai.* Bareilly: Prakash Book Depot, 1986. 159-162.

(ii) Special Issues

Journal of Indian Writing in English 9.1 (1981). Special Number: Anita Desai: The Woman and the Novelist.

Language Forum 14.1 (1988). Special Issue on Anita Desai. Also published in the form of a book under the title, *The Fiction of Anita Desai* edited by R.K. Dhawan. New Delhi: Bahri Publications, 1989.

(iii) Book and Journals

Abrams, M.H. *A Glossary of Literary Terms.* (1993). Bangalore: Prism Books Pvt. Ltd., 1985.

Amanuddin, Syed. "Anita Desai's Technique." *Language Forum* 14.1 (1988). 154-164

Amin, Amina. "Imagery as a Mode of Apprehension in Anita Desai's Novels." *Littcrit.* 10.1 (1985): 36-45

Amin, Zohra Rizvi. "Anita Desai's Suffering Women." *Statesman* 30 June 1987.

Asnani, Shyam. "The Theme of Withdrawal and Loneliness in Anita Desai's *Fire on the Mountain." JIWE* 9.1 (1981): 81-92.

Bala, Suman. ed. *The Fiction of Anita Desai.* New Delhi: Khosla Publishing House, 2002.

Bande, Usha. *The Novels of Anita Desai.* New Delhi: Prestige Books, 1988.

—— "Childhood in Anita Desai's Novels: A Psychological Interpretation." Dhawan, *Indian Women Novelists* Set I. Vol. 2. 101-26. Subsequently cited as Dhawan".

Banerjee, Uma. "An Existential Approach to Maladjustment in Marital Relations in Anita Desai's Novels," Dhawan Set I. Vol. 2. 155-76.

Beauvoir, Simone de. *The Second Sex* [Trans. H.M. Parshley] Hammondsworth: Penguin Books Ltd., 1984.

Beliappa, Meena. *The Fiction of Anita Desai.* Calcutta: Writers' Workshop, 1971.

Bhatnagar, M.K. ed. *Indian Writing in English.* Vol. 1. New Delhi: Atlantic Publishers, 2001.

Bhatnagar, M.K. and M. Rajeshwar. eds. *Indian Writings in English.* Vols. 5-9. New Delhi: Atlantic Publishers and Distributors, 2000.

—The Novels of Anita Desai: A Critical Study. *New Delhi:* Atlantic Publishers and Distributors, 2000.

Chakranarayan, Mohini. *Style Studies in Anita Desai.* New Delhi: Atlantic Publishers, 2000.

Chary, Brahmananda. "Raka as a Metaphor for Ruined Childhood in Anita Desai's *Fire on the Mountain.*" In Bhatnagar and Rajeswar eds., *The Novels of Anita Desai: A Critical Study.* 88-95.

Chaudhury, Bindulata. *Women and Society in the Novels of Anita Desai.* New Delhi: Creative Books, 1995.

Concilio, Carmen. "Anita Desai's *Fire on the Mountain* and the Iconography of the Crone." In *IWE 7,* 120-138.

Conde, Mary. "Women Inscribing the Indian Landscape," *The Atlantic Review,* 1: 2, 2000.

Costa, Magda "Interview with Anita Desai," *Lateral* March 2001 [taken on 30 January 2001, in Barcelona, and originally published in Spanish. The English version is now available online]

Crane, R. "Kicking against the Pricks: Anita Desai's *Fire on the Mountain, Commonwealth and American Women's Discourse: Essays in Criticism* [Ed. A.L. McLeod]. New Delhi: Sterling Publishers, 1996

Cruicksank, John. *Albert Camus and the Literature of Revolt.* London: Penguin Books, 1960.

Dalmia, Yosodhara, "An interview with Anita Desai." *Times of India* 29 August 1979.

Das, Bijay. "Women in Itrospection: A Study of Anita Desai's *Fire on the Mountain." Creative Practice* 3.1 (1996): 35-40.

Das, Sandhyarani. *Form and Vision in the Novels of Anita Desai.* New Delhi: Prestige Books, 1996.

Davidson, Harriet. "Adrienne Rich's Politics and Poetics of Location." *Contemporary Theory Meets Modern Poetry* [Eds. Easthope and Thompson] N.Y.: Harvester Wheatsheaf, 1991.

Desai, Anita. *Fire on the Mountain.* London: Penguin Books,
1977.

Dhawan, R.K., ed. *Indian Women Novelists,* Set I, Vols. 23 & 4; Set II. Vol. 1; Set III. Vols. 1 & 2. New Delhi: Prestige, 1993. Set I, Vols. 2, 3 & 4 are entirely devoted to Anita Desai.

Dodiya, J., ed. *Critical Essays on Anita Desai's Fiction.* New Delhi: Ivy Publishing House, 2000

Findley, Alan H. "Indo-Anglian Literature: A Reading of Anita Desai's *Fire on the Mountain."* Proceedings of the Third Nordic Conference for English Studies. Ishrat Lindblad and Magnes Ljung. Stockholm: Almgvist and Wiksell, 1987.

Gabriele, Anna. "Flight from Matriarchy." Rev, of *Fire on the Mountain. Times Literary Supplement* 17 June 1977.

Ganguli, Chandra. *"Fire on the Mountain:* an Analysis." *Commonwealth Quarterly* 21 (1981): 40-44.

Goel, Kunj Bala. *Language and Theme in Anita Desai's Fiction.* Jaipur: Classic Publishing House, 1989

Gopal, N.R., *A Critical Study of the Novels of Anita Desai.* New Delhi: Atlantic Publishers and Distributors, 1999.

Grene, M. *Introduction to Existentialism.* Chicago: Chicago UP, 1950.

Gupta, G.S. Balarama. ed. *Studies in Indian Fiction in English.* Gulbarga: JIWE Publications, 1987.

——"Anita Desai's *Fire on the Mountain: A* Fictional Metaphor of Existentialist Philosophy," in Srivastava 185-89.

Gupta, R.K. *The Novels of Anita Desai: A Feminist Perspective.* New Delhi: Atlantic Publishers and Distributors, 2002.

Hariprasanna, A. "Feminine Consciousness in Anita Desai's *Fire on the Mountain,"* in Dhawan Set III Vol. 2, 96-103.

Hite, Molly *The Other Side of the Story.* New York: Cornell University Press, 1989.

Hollingworth, Leta S. "Social Devices for Impelling Women to Bear and Rear Children." *The American Journal of Sociology* 22 (July 1916).

Imamdar, F.A. "Anita Desai's Prose Style," in Srivastava 91-103.

Indira, B. Anita Desai as an Artist: A Study in Image and Symbol. *New Delhi: Creative Books, 1994.*

Iyengar, K.R.S. *Indian Writing in English* (1962). New Delhi: Sterling Publishers Private Ltd., 1999.

Jain, J. Stairs to the Attic.: The Novels of Anita Desai. *Ghaziabad: Vimal Prakashan, 1987*

——Interview with Anita Desai. *Rajasthan University Studies in English* 12 (1979): 61-69.

Juneja, Renu. "Identity and Femininity in Anita Desai's Fiction." *Journal of South Asian Literature 22.2* (1987): 77-86.

Kakar, Sudhir, *The Inner World: A Psychoanalytic Study of Childhood and Society in India.* New Delhi: OUP, 1981.

Kaufmann, Walter. *Existentialism from Dostoevsky to Sartre.* Cleveland and New York: The World Publishing Company, 1968.

King, Franci. Rev. of Fire on the Mountain. Spectator *15 July* 1978.

Knapp, Bettina. "Rite of Exit: A Jungian Approach to Anita Desai's *Fire on the Mountain." Indian Literary Review 4* (1988): 27-34

Kohli, Suresh. "From Crowds to Solitude." Rev. of *Fire on the Mountain. Indian Literary Review.* 1:2 (June 1978): 44-47.

Krishna, Francine E. "Anita Desai: *Fire on the Mountain." Indian Literature* Sep-Oct, 1982: 58-69.

Krisnaswamy, Santa, "Anita Desai: The Sexist Nature of Sanity." In *The Women in Indian Fiction in English.* New Delhi: Asia Publishing House, 1982.

Kumar, Shib K. "Art and Experience: A Note on Anita Desai as a Short Story Writer." *Essays in Honour ofRamesh Mohan,* Ed. Rizvi. Austria: Institut fur Anglistik und Amerikanistik, 1982.

Kundu, R. "For a 'Space' of Her Own." *Pegasus.* Vol. 1, October 2001: 28-45.

—ed. *Indian Writing in English* Vol. 2 New Delhi: Atlantic

Publishers and Distributors, 2003.

Maini, D.S. "The Achievement of Anita Desai." *Indo-English Literature.* Ed. R.S. Sharma. Ghaziabad: Vimal Prakashan, 1977.

May, Rollo. *Love and Will.* New York: Northern, 1969.

McGabriel. Rev. of Fire on the Mountain. Hindustan Times, *13 November 1977.*

Nagpal, K. Rev. of Fire on the Mountain. Commonwealth Quarterly *13: 55 (1987): 11-23.*

Naikar, Basavaraj. "Marital Disharmony in Anita Desai's Novels." In Tiwari I: 72-81.

Narendra Kumar, V.L.V.N. "Novel as Image: *Fire on the Mountain* as a Tragic Farce." *Literary Criterion* 29.2 (1994): 18-24

—Fits and Misfits: A Study of Anita Desai's Protagonists, Bareilly: Prakash Book Depot, 1996.

Nayak, P.M. and S.P. Swain. "Anita Desai's *Fire on the Mountain:* The Flame within" In Dhawan Set III Vol. 2. 104-09.

Pal, Sashi. "Alienation to Existentialism: A Study of Anita Desai's Novels." *Quest* (Ranchi) 9.1 (1999) 35-39.

Pande, Mrinal. "Women without Man." Rev. of *Fire on the Mountain. Times of India* 18 December 1977.

Pathak, R.S. "Alienated Self in the Novels of Anita Desai," *Language Forum* 14.1 (1988): 17-53.

Pathania, Usha, "The Filial Ties—A Bane: *Fire on the Mountain."* *Language Forum* 14.1 (1988) Language Forum 14.1 (1988): 108-16.

Patil, Ujjala. "Sexual Violence and Death in Anita Desai's *Fire on the Mountain."* In G.S. Balarama Gupta (ed.) *Studies in Indian Fiction in English*

Paul, Pramila and R. Padmanabha Nair. "Varieties of Loneliness in *Fire on the Mountain"* In Dhawan Set I Vol. 3. 216-35.

Philips, K.J. "Ambiguous Tragic Flaw in Anita Desai's. *Fire on the Mountain." International Fiction Review,* 20 November 1977

Polatnick, M. Rivka. "Why Men Don't Rear Children." *Gender Images* [Eds. Schaum, Melita & Connie Flanagan], Boston: Houghton Miflin Company, 1972.

Polit, Katha. Rev. of *Fire on the Mountain. New York Times* Book Review 20 November 1977.

Prasad, Madhusudan. *Anita Desai: The Novelist.* Allahabad: New Horizon, 1982.

Ram, Atma. "An Interview with Anita Desai." *World Literature Written in English,* 16: 1 (April 1977).

Ram Atma and Usha Bande. "Symbolism in Anita Desai's Fire on the Mountain." World Literature Written in English 24.2: 422-427.

Rao, B. Ramachandra. *The Novels of Mrs. Anita Desai: A Study.* Ludhiana: Kalyani, 1977.

Ryan, Michael. *Literary Theory: Practical Introduction.* Oxford: Blackwell Publishers, 1999.

Scott, Leland H. *Child Development.* New York: Rinehart and Winston, 1967

Sethi, Sunil. "Tremendous Changes." Interview with Anita Desai. *India Today,* December 1-15, 1980

Sharma, R.S. "Movement and Stillness in Anita Desai's *Fire on the Mountain." Littcrit 7,* 4.2 (1978): 1-4

—*Anita Desai.* New Delhi: Heinemann, 1981

Srivastava, R.K. ed. *Perspectives on Anita Desai.* Ghaziabad: Vimal Prakashan, 1987.

Subhas. Rev. of Fire on the Mountain. Statesman *9 September* 1979.

Sunder Rajan, Rajeswari. Rev. of *Fire on the Mountain. Book Review* September-October 1978.

Swain, S.P. "Images of Alienation—*A* Study of Anita Desai's Novels." *Indian Writing in English,* Vol. 5. New Delhi: Atlantic Publishers, 1999

—"Note of Existentialism in the Novels of Anita Desai." In *Indian Writing in English,* Vol. 6. New Delhi: Atlantic Publishers and Distributors, 1999: 101-108.

Tiwari, Subha. [ed.] *Critical Responses to Anita Desai.* 2 Vols. New Delhi: Atlantic Publishers and Distributors, 2004.

Vishnu, Ashwini Kumar. "*Fire on the Mountain:* A Critical Response." In Kundu. 81-89

Weir, Ann Lowry. Rev. of *Fire on the Mountain. World Literature Written in English.* 17.2 (1978).